A Guide to
Intentionalism

Slade Curtis

Copyright © 2023 by Slade Curtis

All rights reserved.

No part of this publication may be reproduced, distributed, or transmitted in any form or by any means, including photocopying, recording, or other electronic or mechanical methods, without the prior written permission of the publisher, except in the case of brief quotations embodied in critical reviews and certain other noncommercial uses permitted by copyright law.

Published by Go Give Grow

Library of Congress Cataloging-in-Publication Data is available.

A Guide to Intentionalism / Slade Curtis - 1st ed. p. cm. ISBN 9798395098139

First Edition: April 2023

Printed in the United States of America

10 9 8 7 6 5 4 3 2 1

To obtain permission to use material from this work, please submit a written request to: admin@gogivegrow.org

Disclaimer: The information provided in this book is for general informational purposes only and is not intended as a substitute for professional advice or services. The author and publisher assume no responsibility for any errors or omissions, or for any actions taken in reliance on the information contained herein.

Table of Contents

Chapter 1: Introducing Intentionalism 1

Chapter 2: The Power the Mind 12

Chapter 3: Identify Values by Understanding Principles 35

Chapter 4: Setting & Pursuing Goals with Purpose 56

Chapter 5: The Art of Prioritization 70

Chapter 6: Building Intentional Relationships ... 85

Chapter 7: Nourishing Body & Mind 104

Chapter 8: Overcoming Obstacles 127

Chapter 9: Living with Gratitude 144

Chapter 10: Finding Purpose & Fulfillment 158

Chapter 11: Maintaining Intentionalism 174

Chapter 12: Concluding Thoughts 187

Preface

Before we progress any further into this book, I want to acknowledge that I am not an expert, nor am I perfect at living an intentional life. My experience with Intentionalism has been a deeply personal and life changing experience, and it is through this journey that I have acquired valuable insights and lessons. I am simply a fellow traveler on the path of life, continuously learning and evolving, just like you.

As someone who has personally experienced the benefits of living intentionally, I am motivated to share my knowledge and insights with others who are seeking to lead more fulfilling lives. I believe that by sharing my experiences, I can contribute to a collective understanding of what it means to live with intention and purpose, helping others unlock their true potential and live their lives to the fullest.

Ultimately, my role in this field is not to be an expert, but to be a guide, mentor, and friend to those who are on their own journey toward intentional living. My hope is that, through my writing and teachings, I can inspire others to embrace this way of life and discover the profound joy, meaning, and fulfillment it has to offer.

My Journey

Have you ever felt like life was happening to you instead of you being in control of your own destiny? That's exactly how I felt not too long ago. I was and still am a planner, always striving to build the perfect life yet constantly faced with disappointment when things didn't work out. I felt stuck in a never-ending cycle of frustration, regret, and longing for something more.

As a planner, I would meticulously map out every aspect of my life. I dreamt of ambitious goals and created countless plans, but it seemed as though most of them crumbled right before my eyes. This left me feeling disheartened and questioning my ability to achieve the happiness I sought. I spent countless hours dwelling on the past or envisioning a brighter future, never truly living in the present moment.

My relationships, too, were affected by this state of mind. I found it challenging to connect with others on a deeper level, as I was often preoccupied with my own frustrations and unfulfilled dreams. I yearned for a sense of control and fulfillment but felt increasingly distant from that elusive goal.

Then, I had an epiphany: the root cause of my distress was none other than myself. I had been living life passively, letting the world manipulate me and dictate my path like a marionette, and allowing my happiness or lack thereof, to be determined by external factors. This way of living just never sat right with me and I wanted to change something but didn't know what to do or where to start. That is when I discovered Intentionalism and everything changed.

Intentionalism is about living life on your own terms, with a clear sense of purpose and direction. It is about taking charge of your thoughts, feelings, and actions to create the life you truly desire. It is about being present in the moment and focusing on what truly matters.

Since embracing Intentionalism, my life has transformed in ways I never imagined possible. I've found a level of happiness that had always eluded me. My relationships have blossomed as I've learned to be more present and authentic with those around me. I have become more mindful of my thoughts, emotions, and surroundings, enabling me to make choices that align with my core values and priorities; creating a joyful, passion filled, purposeful existence.

This journey of self-discovery and personal growth has been an incredible experience that I am eager to share with you. My hope is that you too will discover the life-changing power of living with intention and find the happiness and fulfillment you've been searching for, not just in your life, but within yourself.

Let's embark on this adventure to reclaim our lives, break free from the constraints of circumstance, and create the fulfilling lives we are meant to live. Welcome to Intentionalism, where you will finally find, recognize, and be your true self.

Chapter 1: Introducing Intentionalism

"You cannot control what happens to you, but you can control your attitude toward what happens to you, and in that, you will be mastering change rather than allowing it to master you." -Brian Tracy

Have you ever felt like you are drifting through life, without a clear direction or sense of meaning? Or wondered if there is more to life than just going through the motions of work, chores, and entertainment? Have you ever wished you could live more authentically and in alignment with your true self and values?

Now imagine waking up every morning with a clear sense of direction, a deep feeling of fulfillment, and a contagious enthusiasm for life. Imagine living each day with purpose, passion, and power. Imagine being the architect of your destiny, rather than a spectator of your circumstances. This is not a fantasy, this is Intentionalism.

Intentionalism is not a new concept, it is a timeless one with roots in ancient philosophy, psychology, and spirituality. It is the idea that we have the power and responsibility to shape our destiny by being mindful of our thoughts, feelings, and behaviors. By paying attention to what we think, feel, and do, we can align our actions with our aspirations, our choices with our convictions, and our habits with our hopes. Intentionalism is also the belief that we can make a positive difference in ourselves and the world by being clear about our purpose and values. By knowing what matters most to us and why, we can create a life that reflects who we are and what we care about. Intentionalism is not only an idea but a practice of living deliberately and consciously, rather than passively and reactively, and making decisions based on intention, rather than impulse or habit. It is the practice of being proactive, rather than reactive.

My aim is not to tell you what to do or how to live your life, but to invite you to reflect on your intentions and actions, and to encourage you to experiment with new ways of thinking and being with the goal of helping you discover your own path of Intentionalism.

Why is it not already common practice?

If intentional living is so great, why is it not more commonplace? Why do we find ourselves living in autopilot mode and following habits and routines that don't serve us well? Why do we sometimes feel stuck, confused, or unhappy with life?

The answer may not seem simple but it is. Although many factors can seem as though they prevent us from living intentionally, such as external factors like social pressures, cultural norms, and environmental influences, there is only one thing that can prevent us from living intentionally - our mind.

The human mind is an amazing tool that allows us to learn, create, and communicate, however, it can also become a source of suffering if we identify with it too much.

What does it mean to identify with our mind? It means that what you think or feel is who you are and that mind-made stories define your identity and reality.

For example, when someone hurts you, you might think: "I am a victim. He/she doesn't love me. I am worthless. I will never be happy" which makes you then feel sad, angry, depressed, or hopeless. When something goes wrong, your internal monologue may be saying "I am a failure. I can't do anything right. I am stupid. I will never succeed" causing you to feel anxious, frustrated, ashamed, or fearful. When something goes well, you might think: "I am awesome. I can do anything. I am smart. I will always win," making you feel proud, excited, confident, or arrogant. These thoughts and emotions seem real and convincing to you. They seem like the truth about yourself and your life. They seem like your identity and your reality, but they are not. The thoughts and emotions are just temporary phenomena that arise and pass away in your awareness. They are influenced by many factors, such as your past experiences, your beliefs, your expectations, your mood, and your environment. They are not who you really are.

Finding your True Self

If you have ever asked yourself the question: "Who am I really?" you are already on the path of awakening. You are sensing that there is more to you than meets the eye and are feeling a longing for something deeper and more authentic. I don't mean your name, your occupation, your appearance, or your personality, but your true essence. Your true self.

How do you discover who you truly are? How do you access your true essence? The answer is simple but profound. Your true self is found by becoming aware of your awareness.

Eckhart Tolle, a spiritual teacher, said that our true essence is pure consciousness or the awareness that witnesses our thoughts and emotions. He calls it "the Power of Now".

The power of now is the ability to be fully present in each moment without being distracted by thoughts or emotions. It is the ability to access a deeper dimension within yourself that transcends time and space. It is the ability to connect with the essence of who you are and what life is.

When you live in the now, you realize that you are not your mind or your thoughts or emotions. Those are just temporary phenomena that arise and pass away in your awareness but are not who you really are.

You have a choice whether to believe them or not; whether to act on them or not.

Most thoughts and emotions are based on illusions and are false interpretations of reality which create suffering because they contradict the truth. This truth is that you are inherently worthy, that everyone has their own way of expressing love, that life is neutral, etc.

You have an identity beyond form - beyond your body, your mind, and your ego. Your identity is eternal, infinite, and one with all that is.

You are life itself being expressed through form. You are love itself, radiating through form. You are joy itself, celebrating through form.

This realization of self-identity changes everything, from how you see yourself and others to how you see life as a whole. Which has the capacity to free you from fear, guilt, anger, or resentment and fill you with peace, gratitude, compassion, and generosity. This change empowers us to live a life of Intentionalism and live consciously in alignment with our true nature and purpose. To live from a place of love rather than fear. To live from a place of abundance rather than scarcity. To live from a place of service rather than selfishness.

This realization is not reserved for special people or special occasions. It is not dependent on external circumstances or conditions. It is always here and now - within yourself.

All it takes is a shift in attention and intention, from thinking and reacting into being. Start by asking the simple question "Who am I?" Then reflect and actively listen, not with your ears, but with your heart. And then feel - not with your body, but with your soul. And then know - not with your mind, but with your spirit. That is when you can discover who you truly are: pure consciousness, pure love, pure joy, pure being.

Continuing on the path of discovering your true self, it is crucial to delve deeper into understanding the inner workings of your mind and the nature of consciousness. As you embrace the power of now and cultivate mindful awareness, you will begin to recognize the subtle patterns and habits that have shaped your life.

Begin by observing the flow of your thoughts and emotions without judgment or resistance. As you witness them, you'll start to notice the impermanent nature of these mental and emotional states. Like clouds passing through the sky, they come and go, but you, the observer, remain constant. This constant, unchanging awareness is your true self. As you deepen your understanding of this awareness, you will gradually become more proficient at distinguishing your true self from transient thoughts and emotions that occupy your mind. In this state of heightened self-awareness, you will also recognize that you have the power to choose how you respond to your thoughts and emotions. You can decide whether to indulge in negative patterns or cultivate positive habits that support growth and well-being. This newfound sense of agency will enable you to navigate life with greater ease, resilience, and clarity.

As you continue to explore your true nature, take the time to cultivate self-compassion and forgiveness. Recognize that you are a work in progress and that it is natural for the mind to wander and for emotions to arise. Instead of getting caught up in self-judgment or criticism, embrace the process as an opportunity for transformation.

By consistently practicing mindfulness and embracing the power of Now, you will deepen your connection to your true essence, which is the source of unconditional love, peace, and joy.

Discovering your true self is a profound and transformative journey that requires patience, dedication, and the willingness to explore the depths of your consciousness. As you learn to differentiate between your true essence and the fleeting thoughts and emotions that arise within you, you will find yourself living with greater intention, authenticity, and purpose. This is the ultimate gift of self-discovery, and it is within reach for each and every one of us.

Reflection

Self-discovery is an incredible journey that we have just embarked upon together. We've delved into the world of Intentionalism, unearthing the power behind living a life of purpose and authenticity, and laid the foundation for a rich, fulfilling existence.

We've peeled back the layers of our minds, exploring the reasons why we sometimes fall into the trap of living on autopilot. We've discovered that by breaking free from our mind-made stories and focusing on our true essence, we can harness the power of intentionalism to create a life that genuinely reflects our values and aspirations.

As we continue to journey through this book, we will dive deeper into the art of intentional living, learning to prioritize our time and energy, setting meaningful goals, maintaining a sense of balance, building strong, intentional relationships, and much more.

Embracing the principles of Intentionalism will serve as the launchpad for a transformative journey toward self-discovery, personal growth, and a deeper connection with the essence of who we are and what we care about. So, take a deep breath, and dive into the depths of your being. Embrace the wisdom that lies within you. As you discover who you truly are, you will find yourself living a life of intention, love, and joy, and you will inspire others to do the same.

Remember: Intentionalism is the compass that guides us toward a life of purpose and fulfillment, transforming every moment into a deliberate and meaningful step on the journey to our highest potential.

Chapter 2: The Power of the Mind

"Your mind is a powerful thing. When you fill it with positive thoughts, your life will start to change." - Gautama Buddha

In the depths of our uncharted minds, lies a world of untapped potential, a treasure trove of secrets waiting to be unlocked. It is within these depths that we discover the true essence of our existence, the power to transform our lives, and the key to unlocking our greatest potential. As we embark on this journey, prepare to unleash the extraordinary capabilities of your mind, and awaken the possibilities that have been hidden within you, waiting to be set free.

Embracing the principles of Intentionalism means being mindful of the choices being made and aligning them with our values and goals. The power of your mind and the practice of cultivating mindful awareness is the foundation upon which intentional living is built. By developing a deeper connection with your inner self, you'll be better equipped to make conscious, deliberate decisions that honor your values and propel you toward your life's purpose. In this chapter, we will dive into the intricacies of our thoughts and emotions and the role that they play in shaping our reality.

Our minds possess incredible power, capable of creating and destroying, healing and harming, liberating and imprisoning. Harnessing the power of our minds and nurturing mindful awareness allows us to live intentionally, aligning our actions with our true nature and purpose.

As you step into the next phase of your journey, remember that your true essence is always with you, guiding you toward living a life of intention and purpose. Embrace the power of your mind and cultivate mindful awareness to unlock the infinite potential within you and experience the profound impact it can have on your life and the world around you. As you grow and evolve on this path, you'll truly embody the essence of Intentionalism, creating a life rich in meaning, fulfillment, and joy.

The Power of the Mind: A Tool for Transformation

The mind is an extraordinary instrument, wielding immense power over our thoughts, emotions, and actions. It has the ability to shape our reality, influencing how we perceive ourselves, others, and the world around us. As we journey towards living with intention and purpose, it's essential to understand the role our minds play in this transformative process.

The human mind is like a double-edged sword – it has the power to liberate or imprison, to heal or harm, to create or destroy. It is this duality that makes understanding and harnessing its power so crucial to becoming a true Intentionalist. By learning to direct our thoughts and emotions constructively and consciously, we can unleash the full potential of our minds and create a life filled with meaning and fulfillment.

Thoughts shape reality, as they form the basis of our beliefs, values, and attitudes. When we cultivate positive, empowering thoughts, we build a strong foundation for personal growth and success. Conversely, negative, limiting thoughts can create a self-fulfilling prophecy, preventing us from reaching our true potential. It is essential to become aware of our thought patterns and develop the ability to choose thoughts that support our intentions and aspirations.

Emotions, on the other hand, serve as signals that provide valuable information about our current state of being. While emotions can sometimes feel overwhelming and uncontrollable, we can learn to understand and manage them effectively through mindful awareness. By developing a deeper connection with our emotions, we can recognize their underlying messages and use them as tools for self-discovery and growth.

Unlocking the Power of Our Minds

The human mind is an incredible and complex entity, possessing immense potential to shape our experiences, well-being, and achievements. Throughout history, scientists, philosophers, and spiritual teachers have explored the power of the mind, uncovering fascinating insights that reveal our capacity for growth, healing, and transformation.

By understanding and applying four key principles of our mind, we can tap into the vast reservoir of our mental capabilities and actively work towards a life guided by our true essence and purpose.

Principle 1: Embrace Neuroplasticity

Neuroplasticity refers to the brain's ability to change and adapt throughout an individual's lifetime, forming new neural connections and pathways. This demonstrates that people have the capacity to change thought patterns, habits, and behaviors, ultimately re-shaping their reality. For example, people who have suffered from strokes or traumatic brain injuries have been able to regain lost functions by training their brains to rewire and adapt.

You can also harness the transformative power of your mind. By consciously working on altering your thought patterns, habits, and behaviors, you can reshape your reality.

Dr. Jill Bolte Taylor is a neuroanatomist who suffered a stroke in 1996. The stroke was caused by a blood vessel in her brain rupturing, which led to a hemorrhage. During the stroke, Dr. Taylor experienced a unique opportunity to study the brain from the inside out, as she lost the ability to speak, read, write, and even remember basic details about her life.

Despite these challenges, Dr. Taylor was determined to recover and began using knowledge of the brain to help her heal. She relied on neuroplasticity to relearn speech, movement, and other cognitive functions. Through intense therapy and a lot of hard work, Dr. Taylor was eventually able to make a full recovery.

Dr. Taylor's story exemplifies the extraordinary power of neuroplasticity and its profound ability to impact our daily lives. Her determination and dedication to her recovery showcase the potential each of us has to overcome challenges and reshape our realities. By embracing neuroplasticity and applying its principles, we can harness our minds' adaptability to support personal growth, transformation, and the pursuit of our goals. Dr. Taylor's journey serves as a testament to the resilience and strength of the human spirit, inspiring us all to believe in our inherent capacity for change and growth.

Principle 2: Utilize the Power of Belief

The placebo effect demonstrates the power of the mind in influencing our physical well-being. In a scientific experiment testing the effectiveness of a drug, a random group of the population was given a sugar pill or non-active treatment and told it will improve their condition, they more often than not reported experiencing positive effects, even though the treatment itself had no direct impact on their ailment. This phenomenon highlights the role of our thoughts and beliefs in shaping our experiences and well-being. By embracing this principle, you can positively influence your experiences and overall health.

Placebo treatments are often used in medical research as a way to isolate the effects of a treatment from those of the mind's response to the treatment.

In one particular study, several patients with irritable bowel syndrome were given either a placebo pill or no treatment at all. The placebo pill contained no active ingredients, but patients were told that it was a new medication that had been shown to be effective in treating their symptoms.

Interestingly, the patients who received the placebo pill reported significant improvements in their symptoms, even though the pill had no active ingredients. This effect is believed to be due to the power of the mind's response to the treatment. The patients' belief in the effectiveness of the pill may have triggered a release of endorphins, which are natural painkillers produced by the body. Endorphins can reduce pain and promote feelings of well-being, which may explain why patients in the study reported improvements in their symptoms.

This study highlights the incredible influence our mind has, through beliefs and thoughts, on our body's physical symptoms and well-being. By understanding and embracing this power, we can harness our minds to positively impact our experiences and overall health. The mind-body connection plays a crucial role in our lives, and recognizing this interplay allows us to take more control over our health and happiness.

Principle 3: Master Visualization and Mental Rehearsal

Visualization and mental rehearsal have been proven to be effective in enhancing performance in various fields, including sports, music, and public speaking. By mentally rehearsing a specific task or event in great detail, individuals can improve and enhance their skills, abilities, confidence, focus, and performance, often achieving real-world success. By consistently practicing this principle, you can unlock your potential and excel in any endeavor.

Olympic Gold Medalist, Michael Phelps is known to have used visualization extensively throughout his career. He would mentally rehearse his races, imagining himself swimming each stroke with precision and efficiency. He would also visualize himself standing on the podium, hearing the national anthem, and receiving his gold medal. By repeatedly visualizing these scenarios, Phelps was able to create a mental blueprint for success and cultivate a deep sense of confidence and belief in his abilities.

Phelps has described visualization as a critical component of his mental training regime. He believes that by visualizing success, athletes can prepare themselves mentally for any situation and overcome the obstacles that stand in their way.

The story of Michael Phelps and his use of visualization illustrates the immense potential of mental rehearsal in enhancing performance and achieving real-world success. By incorporating visualization into our daily lives, we can not only improve our skills and abilities but also build confidence and resilience in the face of challenges. Phelps' remarkable achievements serve as a reminder that our minds have the power to shape our reality, and by harnessing the power of visualization, we can unlock our full potential and excel in any area of our lives.

Principle 4: Cultivate Mindfulness for Stress Reduction

The practice of mindfulness has been scientifically proven to reduce stress, anxiety, and depression, illustrating the power of the mind in promoting mental well-being. Mindfulness techniques, such as meditation and mindful breathing help individuals cultivate awareness of their thoughts and emotions. This awareness can enable us to respond more consciously and intentionally to life's challenges.

One particular study on this topic was conducted by researchers at the University of Massachusetts Medical School and involved 22 participants who were experiencing high levels of stress. The participants completed an eight-week MBSR (mindfulness-based stress reduction) program, which included weekly group sessions and daily home practice of mindfulness exercises.

At the end of the program, the participants reported significant reductions in stress, anxiety, and depressive symptoms. They also showed improvements in measures of mindfulness, self-compassion, and resilience.

The findings of this study are consistent with previous research that has shown the potential benefits of mindfulness practices in reducing stress and promoting well-being. This study is significant because it demonstrates the potential benefits of MBSR specifically in reducing stress, anxiety, and depressive symptoms. These are common mental health concerns that can have a significant impact on an individual's quality of life. By providing evidence of the effectiveness of MBSR, this study offers a valuable tool for individuals seeking to manage their stress and promote their mental health.

These examples showcase the immense power of the mind in shaping our experiences, well-being, and success. By harnessing this potential and cultivating mindful awareness, we can actively work towards living a more intentional and fulfilling life, guided by our true essence and purpose.

Cultivating Mindful Awareness

The journey to true happiness, peace, and fulfillment begins with a single step: the conscious decision to immerse yourself in the present moment, embrace the rich tapestry of life unfolding before your eyes, and uncover the hidden potential that lies dormant within you. In the following pages, we will explore the art of cultivating mindful awareness; This is an invaluable skill that may not only transform your perception of the world around you but will also unlock the key to a life of harmony, joy, and boundless satisfaction. We will explore the fundamental principles of mindful awareness and provide practical examples and suggestions to help you integrate these principles into your daily life, ultimately guiding you toward a richer, more profound experience of existence.

Imagine a world where each breath is a treasure, every heartbeat a symphony, and every moment an opportunity for growth, learning, and connection. This is the world of mindful awareness, a realm where the incessant chatter of the mind fades away, and the true essence of our being shines forth in all its radiant glory. We will begin our exploration by examining the importance of the present moment, the foundation upon which all other aspects of mindful awareness are built. We will then jump into the art of transcending the ego-driven mind, cultivating the "observer" or "watcher" consciousness, and embracing acceptance and non-resistance.

This journey requires commitment, persistence, and courage, but the rewards are immeasurable. Through the cultivation of mindful awareness, you will not only discover the true essence of who you are but also unleash the infinite potential that resides within you, paving the way to a life filled with happiness, peace, and fulfillment. So, let us take that first step together, and embark on this exhilarating adventure into the depths of our consciousness, where the treasure of mindful awareness awaits.

The Present Moment: The Key to Mindful Awareness

The most fundamental concept is that the present moment is the most important aspect of our lives, and most of our suffering and discontent arise from our minds' preoccupation with the past and future, preventing us from experiencing the peace and joy inherent in the present moment.

Mindful awareness involves cultivating an intimate connection with the present moment by focusing our attention on the here and now. By doing so, we can transcend the incessant mental chatter and find a state of stillness, peace, and presence.

For example: When waiting in line at the grocery store, instead of becoming impatient or lost in thoughts about your to-do list, focus your attention on the present moment. Observe the sounds around you, the feeling of your feet on the ground, or the sensation of your breath.

How to start: Incorporate small moments of present-moment awareness throughout your day by setting reminders or alarms on your phone to prompt you to pause and focus on your breath or surroundings. Practice this during routine activities like brushing your teeth, eating, or walking.

Transcending the Ego-driven Mind

The primary obstacle to mindful awareness is the ego-driven mind, which we characterized by identification with our thoughts, emotions, and personal narratives. The ego- driven mind perpetuates a sense of separateness and keeps us trapped in cycles of suffering, anxiety, and dissatisfaction.

As we talked about earlier, to cultivate mindful awareness, we must recognize that we are not our thoughts or emotions; rather, we are the conscious awareness that underlies them. By consistently practicing this realization, we can detach from our ego-driven mind and access the true essence of our being, which is characterized by presence, peace, and a sense of interconnectedness with all that is.

For example: When faced with a challenging situation at work or in an issue regarding a personal relationship, instead of becoming defensive or reactive, take a step back and observe your thoughts and emotions as they arise. Recognize that they are transient and not the essence of who you are.

How to start: Practice daily mindfulness meditation to develop the skill of detaching from your thoughts and emotions. When confronted with challenges, remind yourself to observe your reactions without identifying with them, enabling you to respond from a place of conscious awareness instead of a reactive state driven by habitual thought patterns and emotions.

Cultivating the "Observer" Consciousness

Another fundamental aspect of mindful awareness is the cultivation of the "observer" or "watcher" consciousness. This involves developing the ability to observe our thoughts and emotions without judgment, attachment, or identification.

To cultivate this observer consciousness, our best bet is practicing mindfulness meditation, which involves focusing our attention on our breath, bodily sensations, or other anchors in the present moment. As thoughts and emotions arise, we simply observe them without becoming entangled in their content. Over time, this practice helps us develop a sense of detachment from our thoughts and emotions, allowing us to access a deeper state of consciousness, which we might characterize by presence and stillness.

For example: When experiencing a strong emotion like anger or sadness, instead of becoming consumed by it, try to observe the emotion as if you were a neutral observer. Notice how the emotion feels in your body and how your thoughts are influenced by it, without becoming attached to the experience.

How to start: Start by incorporating mindfulness meditation into your daily routine, focusing on observing your thoughts and emotions without judgment. When strong emotions arise, remind yourself to adopt the observer perspective and see them as temporary experiences, not as the essence of who you are.

Embracing Acceptance and Non-resistance

Resistance to the present moment is the primary cause of suffering and discontent. By resisting our current circumstances or striving for something different, we perpetuate a sense of dissatisfaction and disconnection from the peace and joy that are inherent in the present moment.

To cultivate mindful awareness, it's imperative to practice acceptance and nonresistance by embracing the present moment as it is, without judgment or the desire to change it. By doing so, we can transcend the ego-driven mind and access the deeper sense of peace and contentment that lies within.

For example: When stuck in traffic, rather than becoming frustrated and resistant to the situation, accept the present moment as it is. Use this time to focus on your breath, listen to a calming podcast, or simply observe your surroundings without judgment.

How to start: Practice acceptance and non-resistance by reminding yourself of affirmations such as resisting the present moment only leads to suffering. In situations that are beyond your control, choose to accept and make the best of them, finding opportunities for growth, learning, or self-reflection.

How Will This Help Me?

This might be new or unfamiliar to many but by following this approach we will be able to easily cultivate presence, peace, and inner freedom. By focusing on the present moment, transcending the ego-driven mind, cultivating the observer consciousness, and embracing acceptance and non-resistance, we can access the deeper essence of our being and experience the transformative potential of mindful awareness in our daily lives.

Mindful awareness can and will be the key to happiness, peace, and fulfillment when practiced intentionally. Here are just some of the many benefits:

Presence in the present moment: The present moment is the only reality we truly have. Focusing our attention on this fact can help us break free from dwelling on past regrets or anxieties about the future, allowing us to experience the richness and fullness of the present moment. When we are fully present, we can find joy and contentment in even the simplest aspects of our lives.

Transcending the ego-driven mind: We are not our thoughts or emotions, but rather the conscious awareness underlying them. This realization helps us transcend the ego-driven mind, which is often characterized by incessant mental chatter, negative self-talk, and a sense of separateness from others. When we transcend the ego, we can access a deeper state of consciousness characterized by stillness, peace, and a sense of interconnectedness with all that is.

Emotional regulation and resilience: Learn to observe thoughts and emotions without judgment or attachment to respond more consciously and intentionally to life's challenges. This emotional regulation fosters greater resilience, as we become better equipped to manage stress, adapt to change, and navigate difficult situations with grace and equanimity.

Acceptance and non-resistance: Embrace acceptance and non-resistance, recognizing that resistance to the present moment is a primary cause of suffering. By accepting the present moment as it is, we can experience greater inner peace and contentment, even in the face of adversity or challenging circumstances.

Enhanced self-awareness and personal growth: Become more in tune with your thoughts, emotions, and bodily sensations. This heightened self-awareness can lead to personal growth, as we gain a deeper understanding of our patterns, triggers, and areas in need of healing or development.

Improved relationships: Become a better listener and communicator in relationships. By being fully present with others, we can connect on a deeper level, fostering empathy, understanding, and compassion.

Greater overall well-being: Research has shown that the practice of mindfulness and mindful awareness can lead to improvements in physical and mental well-being, including reduced stress, anxiety, and depression, as well as enhanced immune function, cognitive performance, and overall life satisfaction.

Reflection

The power of our minds and the cultivation of mindful awareness are essential. The potential to change our thoughts, habits, and behaviors can and will shape the reality we experience if we let it.

The fundamental principles that can help us harness this potential include being present in the moment, transcending the ego-driven mind, cultivating the observer consciousness, and embracing acceptance and non-resistance. By intentionally integrating these principles into our daily lives, we can unlock the keys to happiness, inner peace, and fulfillment.

This is not the end of our journey to become true Intentionalists; rather, it is just the beginning. The practice of cultivating mindful awareness is a lifelong process, one that requires consistent effort, dedication, and self-compassion. As we continue to explore the depths of our inner world, we will undoubtedly face challenges and setbacks along the way. Yet, by persevering and remaining committed to our practice, we can transform these obstacles into opportunities for growth and self-discovery.

The journey toward mindful awareness is a deeply personal and unique one. Each person will experience this process in their own way, and progress is often not linear. However, by remaining open to the insights and wisdom that emerge along the way, we can continue to deepen our understanding of ourselves and our place in the world.

Ultimately, the power of our minds, when harnessed through mindful awareness, can lead us to a greater sense of connection with ourselves, others, and the world around us. By cultivating this awareness, we can become more conscious and intentional in our actions, fostering a life that is guided by our true essence and purpose. In doing so, we can not only transform our own lives but also contribute to the collective awakening of humanity, helping to create a more compassionate, harmonious, and inter- connected world.

Chapter 3: Identifying Values by Understanding Principles

"Your beliefs become your thoughts, your thoughts become your words, your words become your actions, your actions become your habits, your habits become your values, your values become your destiny." - Mahatma Gandhi

Foundational thoughts, beliefs, and values serve as the compass that guides our thoughts, decisions, and actions, ultimately shaping the course of our lives. When we align our lives with our core values, we not only cultivate a deep sense of purpose and fulfillment but also foster a more authentic and happier existence.

Living in accordance with our values and principles enables us to make decisions that reflect our true selves, leading to increased self-awareness, self-esteem, and overall well-being. When we are in harmony with our core beliefs, our lives become imbued with a sense of meaning and direction. In contrast, when we are disconnected from our values or act in ways that contradict our principles, we often experience feelings of discontent, frustration, and internal conflict. Our actions may feel misaligned with our true nature, leading to a sense of dissonance and dissatisfaction.

To embrace the path of intentional living, we must take the time to explore and clarify our personal values and principles. This involves engaging in self-reflection, introspection, and honest evaluation of our beliefs and priorities. By doing so, we can better understand what truly matters to us, allowing us to make more informed and authentic choices in our daily lives. As you learn about and apply this aspect of Intentionalism into your life, you will learn to:

1. Recognize your core values and principles that shape your identity and drive your actions.
2. Understand how your values and principles influence your decision-making and life choices.
3. Identify areas of your life where your actions may be misaligned with your values and develop strategies to realign them for a more authentic and fulfilling life.

4. Create a personal mission statement that reflects your values and principles, serving as a guiding beacon for your life's journey.
5. Cultivate the habit of regularly reflecting on your values and principles, ensuring they continue to evolve and remain relevant as you grow and change.

By understanding and honoring these foundational beliefs, you will be better equipped to navigate life's challenges and triumphs, ultimately leading to a more authentic, happier, and fulfilling existence.

Values vs. Principles

Stephen R. Covey makes a clear distinction between values and principles best in his book: "The 7 Habits of Highly Effective People."

Covey defines principles as "fundamental truths that have universal application." Principles are timeless and apply to everyone, regardless of their culture, background, or beliefs. Examples of principles include honesty, integrity, fairness, and respect for others.

On the other hand, values are defined as "the subjective, often culturally conditioned, judgments that people make about the relative worthiness of things." In other words, values are the beliefs and ideals that we hold about what is important in life, and they can vary from person to person or culture to culture.

Values can be subjective and sometimes even conflicting. For example, one person might value hard work and achievement above all else, while another might value family and relationships more highly. Principles, on the other hand, are objective and provide a framework for making ethical and effective decisions.

This explanation emphasizes the importance of identifying our core values and principles and aligning our behavior with those principles. By doing so, we can create a strong sense of purpose and meaning in our lives and make decisions that are consistent with our beliefs and values.

Overall, Covey's distinction between values and principles highlights the importance of having a clear set of guiding principles to help us make ethical and effective decisions, regardless of our personal values or cultural background.

Values strongly shape how we interact with the world around us. In essence, our values are the foundation of our identity and determine the kind of person we aspire to be. Aligning our actions with our values is vital for several reasons:

1. Authenticity and integrity: Living in alignment with our values helps us to remain true to ourselves and maintain integrity in our actions. When our behavior is consistent with our values, we are able to express our authentic selves and create a sense of congruence between our inner beliefs and outward actions. This authenticity fosters trust, respect, and credibility, both with ourselves and with others.
2. Personal fulfillment and satisfaction: When our actions align with our values, we experience a greater sense of fulfillment and satisfaction in life. We feel a sense of purpose and meaning, knowing that our choices are contributing to our overall well-being and aligning with our

core beliefs. This can lead to increased self-esteem, confidence, and overall happiness.

3. Better decision-making: Values serve as a guide for decision-making, helping us to navigate complex situations and make choices that are consistent with our beliefs and priorities. When we are clear about our values, we can make more informed and intentional decisions, ensuring that our actions support our long-term goals and aspirations.

4. Improved relationships: Aligning actions with values can lead to healthier and more authentic relationships. When we communicate and interact with others from a place of integrity and authenticity, we foster trust, understanding, and mutual respect. This can lead to deeper connections and more satisfying interpersonal interactions.

5. Greater resilience: Living in alignment with our values can also contribute to greater resilience in the face of adversity. When we are grounded in our values, we have a solid foundation from which to face life's challenges and navigate

difficult situations. This can help us to maintain our sense of purpose and direction, even when confronted with obstacles and setbacks.

Research has shown that values have a significant impact on behavior and decision-making. Many psychological theories and models of human behavior are based on the premise that values are central to understanding how people think, feel, and act.

One of the most well-known theories that emphasize the importance of values in behavior and decision-making is the Theory of Planned Behavior (TPB). The TPB proposes that behavior is a function of three key factors: attitude towards the behavior, subjective norms (i.e., beliefs about what others expect of us), and perceived behavioral control (i.e., our sense of confidence in our ability to carry out the behavior). Attitude towards the behavior is, in turn, shaped by our values and beliefs about the behavior.

Similarly, Self-Determination Theory (SDT) posits that values are central to our sense of autonomy and personal agency. According to SDT, people are most motivated and engaged when they are able to pursue activities that are aligned with their core values and beliefs.

In addition to these theories, research has also shown that values can influence our decision-making in several ways. For example, a study published in the Journal of Consumer Research found that people are more likely to choose products and brands that are consistent with their values, even if they are more expensive or less convenient.

The research on values and behavior suggests that our values play a critical role in shaping how we think, feel, and act. Therefore, we should focus on developing a strong sense of self, based on our core values and principles.

Unfortunately, many people get caught up in external factors such as social status, wealth, or power, and neglect the internal factors that truly define who we are as individuals.

By intentionally choosing values that align with core principles, and by living in accordance with our values and principles, we can create a sense of purpose and meaning in our lives and achieve true success and fulfillment.

Aligning Actions with Values Leads to Greater Fulfillment & Satisfaction

Core values and principles affect every aspect of life; by aligning behavior with values, we can create a sense of purpose and meaning in our lives and achieve greater fulfillment and satisfaction.

One way that identifying and aligning with values can lead to greater fulfillment is by providing a sense of direction and purpose. When we know what we value most, we can focus our time and energy on activities and pursuits that are consistent with those values. This can help us feel more motivated and engaged and give us a sense of direction in our lives.

For example, if someone values creativity and self-expression, they might choose to pursue a career in the arts or start their own creative business. By aligning their behavior with their values, they can create a sense of purpose and fulfillment in their work.

Similarly, when we align our behavior with our values, we can experience a greater sense of authenticity and self-awareness. When our actions and decisions are consistent with our values, we can feel more confident and secure in who we are as individuals leading to greater satisfaction and happiness in our personal and professional lives.

Another way that identifying and aligning with values can lead to greater fulfillment is by helping us establish meaningful relationships with others. When we share similar values with others, we are more likely to connect on a deeper level and build strong relationships. This can provide a sense of belonging and community, which is a fundamental human need.

For example, if someone values honesty and integrity, they are likely to seek out relationships with people who share those values. By aligning their behavior with their values, they can build trust and respect with others, which can lead to more fulfilling and meaningful relationships.

Finally, identifying and aligning with values can help us make ethical and effective decisions. When we have a clear set of guiding principles, we can make decisions that are consistent with our values and beliefs. This can help us feel more confident and secure in our decisions and reduce feelings of guilt or regret.

For example, if someone values environmental sustainability, they might choose to live a more eco-friendly lifestyle and make decisions that are consistent with that value. By aligning their behavior with their values, they can make a positive impact on the world and feel more fulfilled and satisfied with their choices.

Overall, identifying and aligning with values can have a significant impact on our sense of fulfillment and satisfaction in life. By focusing on what we truly value and aligning behaviors with those values, we can create a sense of purpose and meaning, establish meaningful relationships with others, and make ethical and effective decisions.

From Principles to Practice: Aligning Actions with Values

As mentioned above, Stephen R. Covey emphasizes the importance of core principles, fundamental truths that have universal application. How does one go about identifying values based on core principles?

One approach is to reflect on past experiences that have been particularly meaningful or fulfilling and identify the values that were at play in those experiences. For example, if someone had a fulfilling experience volunteering for a cause they believe in, they might identify values such as compassion or community involvement as being important to them. Another approach is to create a list of values and prioritize them based on their importance. This list can include values such as honesty, responsibility, creativity, personal growth, or spirituality. By prioritizing these values, we can better understand what we truly value and how we can align our behavior with those values. A couple more approaches include:

Identifying your "non-negotiables": These are the values that you consider to be so important that you would not compromise them for anything. Examples of non-negotiables might include honesty, integrity, or loyalty. By identifying these core values, you can ensure that you are making decisions and living your life in a way that is consistent with them.

Considering what you stand for: Think about the issues or causes that are important to you. This might include social justice, environmentalism, or animal rights. By understanding what you stand for, you can identify the values that underpin those beliefs and align your life around them.

Reflecting on your role models: Think about the people you admire and look up to. What values do they embody? By identifying the values that you admire in others, you can gain insight into your own core values and how to align your behavior with them.

Once we have identified our personal values, the next step is to align our behavior with those values and principles. This means making intentional choices that are consistent with our values, even when it may be difficult or uncomfortable. For example, if someone values honesty and integrity, they might choose to speak up when they see someone being treated unfairly or to admit when they have made a mistake.

To ensure that your actions align with your values, it is important to engage in regular self-reflection and introspection. Consider the following steps for assessing your behavior:

Identify your core values: Reflect on and clarify principles and beliefs that are most important to you. Write them down and keep them visible as a constant reminder of what you stand for.

Assess your current actions: Evaluate current behaviors, habits, and choices to determine whether they are in alignment with your values. Be honest with yourself and identify any areas where you may be experiencing dissonance or inconsistency.

Set goals and intentions: Based on your assessment, set goals and intentions for how you can better align your actions with your values. Create a realistic and achievable plan for implementing these changes and commit to making them a priority in your life.

Monitor your progress: Regularly assess your progress and make adjustments as needed. Celebrate your successes, learn from your setbacks, and remain committed to your journey of personal growth and alignment.

It is important to remember the last step. Values can change over time as we grow and develop as individuals. Therefore, it is important to regularly reflect on our values and make adjustments as necessary.

To align behaviors with our values, surround yourself with people who share similar or the same values and support your efforts to align behaviors with those values. By surrounding ourselves with like-minded individuals, we can create a sense of community and support that can help us stay aligned with our values.

Recognizing and aligning with our core values and principles is crucial for cultivating a purposeful and fulfilling life. By engaging in exercises and strategies such as determining non-negotiables, reflecting on role models, and participating in values clarification exercises, we can deepen our understanding of the values that truly define us. By setting goals, assessing our decisions, surrounding ourselves with like-minded individuals, and consistently reflecting on our values, we can ensure that our lives are genuinely aligned with these values, fostering a sense of purpose and meaning.

Personal Mission Statement

After gaining a deep understanding of our values and principles, it is essential to have a tangible way to ensure that we maintain consistency in living according to those values. One powerful tool, as taught by Stephen Covey, that can help us achieve this is the creation of a personal mission statement. A personal mission statement serves as a guiding compass, providing direction and focus as we navigate the journey of life.

This mission statement is a concise declaration of our core values, principles, and aspirations. It encapsulates our purpose and vision for our lives, acting as a constant reminder of what we stand for and what we seek to achieve. By crafting a personal mission statement, we create a framework for making decisions and setting goals that align with our values. To create your personal mission statement, consider using the following steps:

Reflect on your core values: Begin by revisiting the values and principles you have identified as most important to you. Consider which of these values is essential to include in your mission statement.

Envision your ideal life: Think about what you want to achieve in your life, both personally and professionally. What kind of person do you want to be? How do you want to impact the world? Consider how your core values can guide you in realizing this vision.

Craft your statement: Combine your core values and your vision for your life into a clear, concise statement. This statement should serve as a guiding principle that you can use to make decisions and set goals that align with your values. Remember to keep it brief (between 2-3 sentences), as a shorter statement will be easier to recall and apply in your daily life.

Review and refine: Once you have created your personal mission statement, take some time to reflect on it. Does it accurately represent your values and aspirations? If not, revise it until it feels authentic and inspiring.

Commit to your statement: Make a commitment to live according to your personal mission statement. Keep it visible in a place where you can see it daily, such as on your desk or as a background on your phone, to serve as a constant reminder of your guiding principles.

Regularly review and adjust: As we evolve and grow in our journey towards becoming more intentional, it is essential to regularly review our personal mission statement and adjust when necessary. Set aside time on a monthly basis to assess whether your mission statement still aligns with your current values and aspirations. As you change and develop as an individual, your mission statement may need to be updated to reflect your evolving priorities and goals.

Creating and committing to a personal mission statement serves as a powerful tool for living a life that is aligned with our values and principles. By regularly reviewing and updating our mission statement, we can ensure that we are continually evolving and adapting to our changing needs and aspirations, ultimately leading to a more intentional, fulfilling life.

To better understand this concept, let's use Alex as an example. After much reflection, Alex has determined that his most important values are integrity, family, and lifelong learning. He wants to create a personal mission statement that will guide his decisions and actions in various aspects of his life.

Alex starts by imagining the kind of person he wants to be and the legacy he wants to leave behind. He envisions himself as an honest and trustworthy individual who can be relied upon by friends, family, and colleagues. He sees the importance of nurturing and maintaining strong relationships with his family, spending quality time with them, and supporting them through life's challenges. Alex also wants to cultivate a mindset of continuous learning and growth, staying curious and open to new ideas. With these principles in mind, Alex creates his mission statement:

"To live a life of unwavering integrity, to cherish and support my family, and to continuously seek wisdom and growth in all areas of life."

To stay true to his mission statement, Alex incorporates his values into his daily routine. He ensures that he speaks truthfully and takes responsibility for his actions. He makes time for family dinners, attends his children's events, and schedules regular date nights with his spouse. Alex also dedicates time each week to read, attend workshops, and engage in intellectual discussions with friends and colleagues.

Alex reviews his mission statement monthly to make sure it remains aligned with his values and priorities. As Alex's values evolve and he discovers the importance of community service and physical well-being, he decides to update his personal mission statement to reflect these new priorities. His updated mission statement reads:

"To live a life of unwavering integrity, to cherish and support my family, to continuously seek wisdom and growth in all areas of life, to actively contribute to the betterment of my community, and to prioritize my physical well-being for a balanced and healthy life."

By incorporating community service and physical well-being into his mission statement, Alex ensures that these aspects of his life receive the attention they deserve. He may volunteer at a local food bank or organize neighborhood cleanups to give back to his community, and he might also establish a regular exercise routine and make healthier food choices to maintain his physical health. By regularly reviewing and updating his mission statement, Alex continues to live a life that is aligned with his values, leading to greater fulfillment and satisfaction.

By crafting and living by and then regularly reviewing and updating his personal mission statement, Alex is able to make decisions and take actions that align with his core values. This intentional approach to life allows him to create a meaningful, fulfilling existence that reflects his true character and contributes to his overall happiness and well-being.

Chapter 4: Setting & Pursuing Goals with Purpose

"The greater danger for most of us isn't that our aim is too high and we miss it, but that it is too low and we reach it." – Michelangelo

Previously, we discussed the power of our minds, the importance of cultivating mindful awareness, and the role of aligning our actions with our values. Now we will build on the foundation we have made and discuss the process of setting and pursuing goals purposefully, guided by the principles of Intentionalism.

Establishing goals is a critical aspect of Intentionalism, as it enables us to take proactive steps toward creating the life we desire. By setting goals that align with our values and priorities, we can devise a roadmap for our lives that keeps us on track and ensures our choices remain intentional. This chapter will explore the various aspects of goal setting and illustrate how it can support our journey toward intention- al living.

Benefits of Purposeful Goal Setting

Setting and pursuing goals with purpose has numerous advantages that contribute to the success of intentional living. One of the key benefits is the opportunity for personal growth and development. When we establish goals for personal growth and development, we challenge ourselves to step beyond our comfort zones and acquire new skills and abilities. This process can lead to increased confidence, improved self-esteem, and a stronger sense of personal empowerment.

Purposeful goal setting also promotes self-reflection and self-improvement. By identifying areas where we need to grow and developing strategies for overcoming obstacles, we can achieve our desired outcomes. Setting goals with purpose enhances our sense of direction and meaning and can improve our decision-making skills. When we have clear goals in mind, it becomes easier to evaluate the choices we make and ensure they contribute to our long-term objectives. This deliberate decision-making process can lead to a more fulfilling and intentional life.

Setting and pursuing goals with purpose can lead to a greater sense of achievement and satisfaction. When we accomplish the goals that align with our values and priorities, we experience a deep sense of accomplishment and contentment, knowing that our efforts have been meaningful and intentional.

Ultimately, goal setting is a vital aspect of intentional living and plays a significant role in the journey toward becoming an Intentionalist. By setting and pursuing goals that align with our values and priorities, we can take proactive steps towards achieving the life we desire, create a roadmap that keeps us on track, and make intentional choices. Whether it's improving our health, pursuing a personal passion, or achieving a career milestone, setting and achieving meaningful goals can help us live with greater purpose and intention, supporting our personal growth and development.

Gaining Clarity in Your Goals

As an Intentionalist, gaining clarity in goals is paramount to living a life that aligns with your values and priorities. Cultivating a deep understanding of your objectives sets the stage for making intentional choices. The process of clarifying goals can be challenging. To guide you through this step, here are several tips to help you gain clarity and establish goals that truly resonate with your life's vision:

Discover your values: Before setting any goals, take the time to identify your core values. These guiding principles serve as the foundation for your decisions and behaviors. Reflect on what matters most to you and what you want to prioritize in your life.

Visualize your aspirations: A vision board is a powerful tool for representing your goals and aspirations in a tangible, visual way. Collect images, quotes, and other visuals that symbolize your dreams and aspirations to help maintain focus and motivation.

Focus on the bigger picture: Always consider the long-term impact of your goals. What lasting achievements do you hope to accomplish? How do your goals align with your overall vision for your life?

Be specific and concrete: A clear goal is a specific goal. Instead of setting a vague objective like "be healthier," strive for a more concrete target such as "exercise for 30 minutes a day, five days a week." Specificity enables you to better understand what you're aiming for and increases your chances of success.

Break it down into manageable steps: Once you have established goals, divide them into smaller, achievable tasks. This approach keeps you motivated and focused, preventing you from feeling overwhelmed by the enormity of your aspirations.

Make it measurable: Establishing measurable goals allows you to track your progress effectively. By quantifying your achievements, you can maintain motivation, celebrate your successes, and adjust your goals as necessary.

Write it down: The simple act of writing down your goals can help solidify them in your mind and reinforce their importance. Use a journal or planner to record your goals and track your progress.

By following these tips, you'll gain clarity in your goals and move closer to a life of Intentionalism. Remember that setting and achieving goals is an ongoing process that requires patience and persistence.

With clarity, focus, and dedication to intentional living, you'll be well-equipped to accomplish anything you set your mind to.

With a newfound clarity in your goals, you're one step closer to living a truly intentional life. Now it's time to ensure your aspirations are not only clear but also deeply rooted in your values and priorities. In doing so, you'll create a strong foundation for a life that's not only fulfilling but also true to who you are.

Setting Goals to Align with Values & Priorities

Once you have identified your values and priorities, it's time to set goals that align with these guiding principles. By establishing goals that reflect your values, you can ensure that your actions and decisions are purposeful and intentional, ultimately contributing to your overall sense of fulfillment and satisfaction. To create and set goals that align with your values and priorities, consider the following steps:

Choose SMART goals: Set goals that are Specific, Measurable, Achievable, Relevant, and Time-bound. By doing so, you'll have well-defined, quantifiable, and realistic objectives that align with your values and have a clear timeline for completion.

Prioritize your goals: Evaluate the importance and urgency of each goal and prioritize them accordingly. This will help you to allocate your time and resources effectively, ensuring that your most important goals are given the attention they deserve.

Developing a Plan of Action for Achieving Goals

With your value-aligned goals in place, the next step is to develop a comprehensive plan of action for achieving these objectives. By adopting a structured and systematic approach to goal attainment, you can enhance your chances of success and maintain focus on your priorities. Consider the following 4 steps when crafting your plan of action:

1. **Identify resources and support**

List potential resources: Create an inventory of the tools, resources, and support systems that may be necessary for achieving your goals. This may encompass financial resources, educational materials, professional guidance, or the assistance of friends and family.

Assess your current resources: Evaluate your existing resources and determine whether they are sufficient for achieving your goals, or if additional resources need to be acquired.

Develop a network: Connect with individuals or organizations that share your values and goals. These connections can provide valuable insights, advice, and support as you work towards your objectives.

2. Establish a timeline and milestones

Break down your goals: Divide your overarching goals into smaller tasks or objectives, organizing them into a logical sequence.

Set deadlines: Assign specific deadlines for each task or objective, ensuring that they are realistic and attainable.

Establish milestones: Identify significant milestones along your journey toward achieving your goals. These milestones will serve as markers of progress and opportunities to celebrate your achievements.

3. Monitor your progress

Establish a tracking system: Implement a system for tracking your progress toward your goals, whether it's a spreadsheet, journal, or project management tool.

Schedule regular check-ins: Set aside time for regular check-ins on your progress, such as weekly or monthly reviews. Use these sessions to assess your progress, identify areas for improvement, and make any necessary adjustments to your plan.

Learn from setbacks: Embrace setbacks or obstacles as opportunities for growth and learning. Reflect on the challenges you encounter and develop strategies for overcoming them in the future.

4. Remain flexible and adaptable

Be open to change: Acknowledge that circumstances may change as you work towards your goals, requiring you to adapt and modify your plans accordingly.

Review and revise: Periodically review your goals and plans to ensure they remain relevant and aligned with your values and priorities. Be prepared to revise your strategies and objectives as needed.

Maintain a growth mindset: Cultivate a mindset that embraces change, learning, and growth. This mindset will enable you to adapt more readily to unforeseen challenges and capitalize on new opportunities that may arise along your journey.

By following these in-depth steps and strategies, you can develop a robust plan of action that will guide you in the pursuit of your goals. This comprehensive approach ensures that you are well-prepared and equipped to face the challenges and opportunities that may emerge as you strive for personal and professional growth.

Having Presence in the Present: Embracing Mindfulness in Goal Setting

Living intentionally involves more than just setting and pursuing goals. It requires cultivating a sense of presence and mindfulness, even as you work towards your aspirations. By embracing the present moment, you can better appreciate your journey and make more conscious decisions that align with your values and priorities. Here are some strategies to help you stay present while goal setting:

Start with a mindful foundation: Begin each goal-setting session by taking a few deep breaths and centering yourself in the present moment. Clear your mind of distractions and focus on the here and now. This mindful foundation will help you approach your goal-setting process with intention and presence.

Embrace the journey: Recognize that the process of working towards your goals is just as important as the outcomes you seek. By embracing the journey and finding joy in the present moment, you can maintain a balanced perspective and avoid becoming overly fixated on future achievements.

Listen to Your Intuition: As you set and pursue your goals, maintain an open and receptive mindset. Listen to your inner voice and trust your instincts. By doing so, you'll stay connected to the present and make more authentic decisions that truly align with your values and priorities.

Cultivate Gratitude: Make it a habit to express gratitude for your current circumstances, the progress you've made, and the opportunities that have come your way. By fostering a sense of gratitude, you anchor yourself in the present moment and create a positive mindset that supports your goal-setting endeavors, even as you plan and strive for a better future.

Savor small victories: Don't forget to acknowledge and celebrate small achievements along the way toward your bigger goals. By recognizing these accomplishments, you remind yourself of the progress you're making in the present, keeping you motivated and connected to the journey.

Stay flexible and open to change: Be prepared to adapt and adjust your plans in response to the ever-changing present moment. By remaining open and receptive to change, you can better navigate the uncertainties of life and maintain a healthy balance between present-moment awareness and future-oriented planning.

Find Balance: Strive to find a balance between focusing on your goals and enjoying the present moment. Recognize that life is a delicate dance between planning for the future and embracing the now. By maintaining this balance, you'll experience a deeper sense of fulfillment and purpose throughout your journey.

Practice Mindful Reflection: Regularly set aside time for mindful reflection. During these sessions, focus on your thoughts and feelings related to your goals. This practice will help you maintain a connection to the present moment and enable you to make any necessary adjustments to your goals and plans.

By incorporating these strategies into your goal-setting process, you'll stay grounded in the present moment and live a more intentional, mindful life.

Reflection

By identifying our values and priorities, setting goals that align with these guiding principles, and developing a plan of action, we can create a purpose-driven life that reflects our authentic selves.

Setting and working towards goals is an essential component of living a life of Intentionalism requiring patience, persistence, and dedication. Clarifying goals gives direction and purpose to our lives. Goal setting is a process and it takes time, effort, and commitment to achieve our objectives. Celebrating progress made along the way and reflecting on successes and challenges can help us stay motivated and make adjustments to our goals as needed.

Chapter 5: The Art of Prioritization

"You will never find time for anything. If you want time, you must make it." – Charles Buxton

In today's fast-paced world, we often find ourselves juggling numerous tasks, striving to meet deadlines, and over-working to achieve goals. Amidst this whirlwind of activities, it is crucial to recognize the importance of prioritizing our time and energy. In this chapter, we will dive into the art of focusing on what truly matters, eliminating time-wasting habits, and cultivating strategies to use our time and energy efficiently. We will also explore practical tips to prevent burnout.

The Science Behind Time-Wasting & Procrastination

We've all been there – sitting down to complete an important task only to find ourselves sucked into a vortex of social media, random internet browsing, or some other seemingly urgent distraction. Time-wasting habits and procrastination are universal challenges that plague many people, but have you ever wondered what's happening in our brains when we fall into these traps? Let's explore the psychological and emotional processes that drive our time-wasting behaviors and procrastination habits. By understanding the behind-the-scenes of these habits, we can better equip ourselves to overcome them.

Unraveling the Emotional Roots of Procrastination

At its core, procrastination is rooted in our emotions. When faced with tasks that trigger discomfort, anxiety, or overwhelm, our brains naturally seek short-term relief by gravitating toward distractions that offer instant gratification. This emotional response is the mind's way of prioritizing the present over the future, protecting us from immediate discomfort.

Fear and anxiety are two key emotions that contribute to procrastination. Fear of failure or judgment can prevent us from starting a task, as the mind perceives potential negative outcomes or embarrassment as threats. Similarly, anxiety about the difficulty of a task can lead to avoidance, as our brains prefer to escape the source of stress rather than confront it head-on.

Perfectionism, or the belief that we must achieve flawless results, can also contribute to procrastination. When we set unrealistically high standards for ourselves, we create unnecessary pressure. These emotions can paralyze and prevent us from taking action if we fear that our efforts may not meet our expectations.

Low self-efficacy, or a lack of confidence in our ability to complete a task successfully, can contribute to procrastination. When we doubt our competence, we may avoid tasks that we perceive as challenging. The prospect of confronting tasks can elicit feelings of inadequacy or frustration. In turn, we may seek comfort in more enjoyable activities that don't challenge our self-worth.

Guilt can also play a role in perpetuating procrastination. When we procrastinate, we may feel guilty for not accomplishing our tasks or meeting our responsibilities. This guilt can create a vicious cycle: the more we procrastinate, the more guilty we feel, which in turn can lead to further avoidance and procrastination as we try to escape these negative emotions.

The Prefrontal Cortex, located in the front part of our brains, is responsible for high-level cognitive functions like decision making, planning, and self-control. This area of the brain helps us resist the urge to procrastinate by prioritizing tasks and weighing the consequences of our actions. However, when we're stressed or fatigued, our prefrontal cortex's capacity to exert self-control is diminished, leaving us vulnerable to the siren call of distractions and time-wasting activities.

The Dopamine Dilemma: Dopamine, a neurotransmitter linked to pleasure and reward, plays a crucial role in driving our procrastination habits. When we indulge in activities like browsing social media or binge-watching our favorite shows, our brains release dopamine, creating a pleasurable sensation that reinforces these behaviors. This dopamine-driven reward system can make it challenging to resist the temptation to procrastinate.

The Lure of Novelty and the Fear of Missing Out: Our brains are wired to seek out novelty, constantly craving new information and stimuli. In today's digital age, the internet and social media platforms offer an endless stream of engaging content, making it difficult to resist their allure. This constant exposure to new information can create a sense of urgency and a fear of missing out (FOMO), further fueling our procrastination habits as we compulsively check for updates, notifications, or fresh content.

Falling Into the Trap

As humans, we often fall into a variety of time-wasting and procrastination habits, which can significantly impact our productivity and effectiveness. Some common examples include:

1. Social media: Scrolling through social media feeds, engaging in online debates, or mindlessly browsing through photos and videos can consume a substantial amount of time.
2. Binge-watching TV shows or movies: Spending hours watching TV shows, movies, or streaming services can lead to procrastination and reduced productivity.

3. Excessive email checking: Constantly checking and responding to emails can disrupt focus and concentration on more important tasks.
4. Online shopping: Browsing online stores or engaging in impulsive buying can be a significant time waster.
5. Daydreaming: While occasional day dreaming can be beneficial for creativity, excessive daydreaming can interfere with productivity and task completion.
6. Perfectionism: Spending too much time obsessing over minor details or making something perfect can delay progress on other important tasks.
7. Over-planning: Spending excessive time on planning and organizing without taking action can be a form of procrastination.
8. Gossiping and engaging in office politics: Spending time discussing other people's lives or getting involved in workplace drama can lead to wasted time and reduced focus on work.
9. Constantly switching between tasks: Multitasking and frequent task-switching can

be counterproductive, leading to reduced efficiency and focus.
10. Indecision: Spending too much time deliberating over decisions can be a form of procrastination and waste valuable time.
11. Unnecessary meetings: Attending meetings without a clear purpose or agenda can consume time that could be spent on more productive tasks. Playing video games or engaging in other digital distractions: Excessive gaming or using digital devices for non-productive activities can contribute to time-wasting and procrastination.

Awareness is the first step toward change. By identifying the triggers and patterns of our time-wasting behaviors, we can create a more intentional and focused approach to our daily lives. This newfound understanding can empower us to break free from the grip of procrastination and embrace a more productive, purposeful lifestyle.

Combat Time-Wasting Habits and Procrastination

Understanding the science behind time wasting and procrastination behaviors allows us to implement strategies to counteract them. One effective approach is to break tasks into smaller, manageable steps, reducing the feelings of overwhelm and anxiety that often triggers procrastination.

Practicing mindfulness, self-awareness, and presence can help us recognize when we're about to engage in time-wasting activities or procrastination. Acknowledging these feelings and staying present enables us to make a conscious decision to refocus on the task at hand. Creating a prioritized to-do list and assigning specific times for each task can provide structure and reduce the likelihood of procrastination.

Identifying and eliminating common distractions in your environment is another helpful strategy. For example, turn off notifications on your devices, close unnecessary tabs or apps, or create a dedicated workspace. Implementing the Pomodoro Technique, a time management method that breaks work into focused intervals separated by short breaks, can help maintain motivation and focus throughout the day.

By understanding the science behind our procrastination habits, we can take proactive steps to overcome these behaviors. With persistence and determination, we can break free from the shackles of procrastination and unlock our true potential.

Strategies for Prioritizing Time & Energy on What Truly Matters

As we explore the concept of Intentionalism, we can learn to focus on what truly matters, ultimately leading to increased productivity, satisfaction, and fulfillment. This section offers <u>9 strategies</u> inspired by the principles of Intentionalism and essentialism to help you concentrate your time and energy on the most important aspects of your life.

1. Discover Your Intentional Purpose: This is the overarching goal or purpose that guides your life and helps you determine what is truly important. Reflect on your core values and

priorities, and craft a clear statement of your intentional purpose.

2. Discern the Vital Few from the Trivial Many: Intentionalism is about distinguishing the vital few tasks and activities that are most important from the trivial many that are not. Evaluate each task and activity in your life and determine if it aligns with your intentional purpose. Focus your time and energy on the vital few and eliminate or minimize the trivial many.

3. Create Space to Think and Reflect: Creating space to think and reflect on life, priorities, and goals is an essential aspect of Intentionalism. Regularly carve out time for self-reflection and use this space to reassess your priorities and ensure that you are focusing on what truly matters.

4. Apply the 90% Rule: When evaluating tasks, activities, and commitments, if something does not score at least 90% in terms of importance or alignment with your intentional purpose, consider eliminating it. This approach will help

you focus on the most critical tasks and activities in your life.
5. Prioritize Your Daily Tasks: Each day, make a list of your most important tasks, focusing on those that align with your intentional purpose. Limit your list to a manageable number (e.g., three to five tasks), and prioritize these tasks above all others.
6. Learn to Say No: Say no to non-essential tasks and commitments. By declining unnecessary requests, you can preserve your time and energy for activities that truly align with your intentional purpose.
7. Embrace the Power of Trade-offs: Trade-offs are an inherent part of life and embracing them is a key aspect of Intentionalism. Recognize that by choosing to prioritize certain tasks and activities, you are also choosing to deprioritize others. Be intentional about the trade-offs you make and ensure that they align with your intentional purpose.
8. Cultivate Routine and Rituals: Developing routines and rituals can help you maintain focus

on your intentional purpose and consistently prioritize your time and energy. Establish habits that support your intentional purpose, such as a morning routine or a daily planning ritual.
9. Focus on Progress, Not Perfection: Recognize that you will make mistakes and face setbacks but stay committed to your intentional purpose and continue to prioritize your time and energy on what truly matters.

By implementing these strategies based on the principles of Intentionalism, you can focus your time and energy on what truly matters, leading to increased productivity, satisfaction, and fulfillment. Embrace the disciplined pursuit of a purposeful life, and you'll find that your life becomes more intentional, rewarding, and aligned with your core values.

Avoiding Burnout

Balancing work, relationships, and personal growth can be challenging, but embracing intentionalism can help prevent overwhelm and maintain a balanced life. Intentionalism emphasizes focusing on what truly matters, eliminating non-essentials, and actively choosing where to dedicate your time and energy. By prioritizing tasks and commitments that align with your values and contribute to your overall well-being, you can prevent spreading yourself too thin and becoming overwhelmed.

Being present in the moment and practicing mindfulness can alleviate stress and free us from future anxieties and past regrets. Techniques such as meditation or deep breathing exercises can anchor you in the present, allowing you to approach your daily life with a calm and focused mindset.

Managing your time and energy effectively involves learning to say no to non-essential tasks and commitments, as well as setting healthy boundaries. Overextending yourself can lead to burnout and exhaustion, but by communicating your limits and consistently enforcing boundaries, you can maintain a healthier work-life balance.

Prioritizing self-care and scheduling downtime is essential for maintaining your well-being. Allocate time for rest, relaxation, and activities that nourish your mind, body, and spirit, such as exercise, meditation, healthy eating, or engaging in creative pursuits. Downtime can be as simple as taking a walk, enjoying a hobby, or spending quality time with loved ones, but it's crucial to recharge and rejuvenate regularly.

Cultivating gratitude and focusing on what you're grateful for can help shift your perspective from feeling overwhelmed to appreciating the present moment. Develop a gratitude practice, like journaling or reflecting on things you're grateful for each day, to maintain a positive outlook on life.

Finally, don't hesitate to seek support when feeling overwhelmed or burned out. Connecting with friends, family, or professionals who can offer guidance, encouragement, and support is vital for maintaining balance in your life. Remember that seeking help is a sign of strength, not weakness.

Embrace the principles of Intentionalism and mindful living to make the most of each moment. Mastering the art of prioritizing time and energy is an essential aspect of living a life of Intentionalism. As we put these principles into practice, we will experience personal growth, increased clarity, and a sense of inner peace that comes from living in alignment with our true nature. By remaining committed to the principles of Intentionalism, we can continually refine our approach, adapt to the ever-changing landscape of our lives, and thrive in a world that increasingly demands our attention and energy.

With a strong foundation in Intentionalism, we can confidently face the challenges and opportunities that life presents, knowing that we are living our lives with purpose, passion, and authenticity.

Chapter 6: Building Intentional Relationships

"You can make more friends in two months by becoming interested in other people than you can in two years by trying to get other people interested in you." – Dale Carnegie

In this chapter, we will be drawing upon the expertise of renowned authors and thought leaders such as Stephen R. Covey and Dr. Dale Carnegie, who have dedicated their lives to understanding and teaching the art of building meaningful and authentic connections. Picture this: you are surrounded by people who uplift, inspire, and support your growth. They bring out the best in you and help you live a more intentional life. Exciting, isn't it? Well, that's what this chapter is all about – building intentional relationships.

The people we choose to surround ourselves with play a crucial role in shaping our lives. They can either fuel our journey towards Intentionalism or hinder it. In this chapter, we will explore the various types of relationships that support intentional living, learn strategies for cultivating these connections, and tackle the challenging topic of addressing toxic relationships and setting healthy boundaries. Together, we'll unlock the secrets to creating a supportive network that empowers you to live your best, most intentional life!

Relationships that Support Intentionalism

Intentional living is a lifestyle that emphasizes mindfulness, authenticity, and alignment with personal values and priorities. Nurturing relationships that support this way of living can greatly enhance our well-being, personal growth, and overall life satisfaction.

Growth-Oriented Relationships and the Importance of Support

Fostering relationships that encourage personal growth is crucial for intentional living. These connections are characterized by mutual understanding, respect, and a shared commitment to personal development. In a growth-oriented relationship, both individuals challenge and inspire each other to learn, evolve, and become the best versions of themselves. It's essential to surround yourself with people who share your values and are open to growth and change.

At the same time, nurturing supportive relationships provide a safe space for expressing thoughts, feelings, and vulnerabilities. These connections are marked by empathy, compassion, and genuine care for one another's well-being. They offer comfort and reassurance during difficult times and celebrate successes together. Seek out people who genuinely care about you and uplift your spirit.

Accountability and the Role of Mentors

Another key aspect of relationships that supports intentional living is accountability. Having someone to check in with, share your progress, and discuss challenges can help you stay on track and maintain motivation. Accountability partnerships are relationships in which both individuals hold each other responsible for their actions and commitments. Look for individuals who are reliable, goal-oriented, and share a similar commitment to personal growth.

Mentorships and role-model relationships can also provide invaluable guidance and inspiration for intentional living. These individuals have experience and wisdom to share, helping you navigate your personal growth journey more effectively. Mentors and role models can offer insights, advice, and encouragement, supporting you in reaching your goals and realizing your potential. Identify individuals who embody the values that you aspire to and engage with them in meaningful ways.

The Power of Mindful Connections

Intentional living is rooted in being fully present and engaged in each moment. Relationships that foster mindfulness and presence can be incredibly enriching and supportive of this lifestyle. These connections are characterized by deep, intentional conversations, shared moments of stillness, and a mutual appreciation for the present moment. Cultivating connections with individuals who value mindfulness and share a desire to live in the present further enhances the intentional living experience.

Cultivating relationships that support intentional living can significantly enhance our well-being and personal growth. By fostering growth-oriented, nurturing, accountable, inspirational, and mindful connections, we create a supportive environment that allows us to live a purpose-driven life. As we nurture these intentional relationships, we not only enrich our own lives but also contribute positively to the growth and well-being of those around us.

Strategies for Cultivating Intentional Relationships

Cultivating intentional relationships, which align with our values, promote growth, and contribute positively to our lives, requires commitment, effort, and the application of proven principles. By fostering such connections, we support our journey toward a purposeful and fulfilling life.

Developing a genuine interest in others, as emphasized by Dale Carnegie's philosophy, involves showing sincere care and curiosity about people's lives, thoughts, and feelings. Actively listening, asking open-ended questions, and seeking to understand others' perspectives can deepen our connections and form the basis of intentional relationships. Coupled with this is Stephen Covey's principle of "Seek First to Understand, then to be Understood," which stresses the importance of empathy and understanding. By truly grasping others' emotions and experiences, we create a foundation of trust, openness, and authenticity.

Emotional intelligence is a key factor in building intentional relationships, as it enables us to navigate complex interpersonal dynamics, respond empathetically to others' needs, and communicate our feelings and perspectives effectively. By developing emotional intelligence and honing our active listening skills, we foster deeper connections and create more meaningful relationships. These skills, together with a genuine interest in others, allow us to establish a foundation of trust, openness, and authenticity, which is essential for nurturing intentional connections.

Embracing vulnerability, though intimidating, is essential for meaningful relationships. Sharing our thoughts, feelings, and experiences openly allows us to deepen connections and grow together. To ensure our connections flourish, it is necessary to consciously invest time and effort in the relationships that support our intentional living journey, engaging in shared activities and celebrating milestones.

Setting and respecting boundaries is a critical component of maintaining balance and ensuring mutual respect in intentional relationships. Openly communicating needs, limits, and expectations, and respecting others' boundaries promotes trust and understanding. This practice forms a strong foundation for long-lasting connections.

Finally, being open to growth and change within relationships allows us to adapt and evolve together as we navigate life's challenges and opportunities. Supporting and encouraging one another's personal development, celebrating successes, and learning from setbacks lead to truly intentional relationships. By investing in these connections, we not only enhance our own lives but also create a ripple effect of positivity, growth, and connection within our communities.

Recognizing Toxic Relationships

Toxic relationships can be challenging to navigate and have a significant impact on our well-being, making it crucial for us to recognize and address them. These relationships often involve various negative patterns such as manipulation, control, excessive criticism, emotional abuse, or a constant lack of support, all of which can hinder our progress in living an intentional life. One way to identify a toxic relationship is by paying attention to how you feel during or after interacting with certain individuals; if you consistently feel drained, anxious, or belittled, it may be a sign that the relation- ship is unhealthy.

Emotional manipulation is one-way toxicity can manifest, as it occurs when a person uses guilt, fear, or other tactics to control someone else's emotions and actions. This type of manipulation, whether subtle or overt, can undermine an individual's sense of self and autonomy. Another troubling aspect of toxic relationships is the presence of constant criticism or belittling, which erodes self-esteem and creates feelings of inadequacy. Constructive feedback is essential for personal growth, but continuous negative criticism signifies an unhealthy dynamic.

Control is another issue that can arise in toxic relationships, with one person attempting to dictate their partner's decisions, actions, and even thoughts, which can lead to a loss of individuality and autonomy. Emotional neglect may also be a factor, leaving one person feeling consistently and constantly ignored, dismissed, or unsupported by their partner. Furthermore, a healthy partnership should have a balance of giving and receiving support, but in a toxic relationship, an unequal give-and-take dynamic can emerge, leading to emotional exhaustion for one party.

It's important to remember that these signs are not exhaustive, as each individual's experience with toxic relationships may differ. Trusting your instincts and paying attention to how your relationships impact your well-being is crucial, as your intuition can serve as a guide in identifying toxic patterns and behaviors. By recognizing and addressing these unhealthy dynamics, we can take steps to improve or remove toxic relationships from our lives and focus on fostering connections that align with our values and intentions.

Addressing Toxic Relationships and Setting Boundaries

The quality of our relationships significantly influences our overall life experience. Surrounding ourselves with nurturing, supportive connections help us stay aligned with our purpose and values. Toxic relationships can hinder our growth and drain our energy, making it difficult to live intentionally.

Toxic relationships often involve patterns of emotional manipulation, constant criticism, control, neglect, or other behaviors that negatively impact our self-esteem and emotional health. These relationships can leave us feeling trapped, unsupported, and disconnected from our true selves. To fully embrace intentional living, it is essential to recognize and address these toxic relation- ships and establish healthy boundaries that protect our well-being and support our personal growth.

Setting boundaries not only helps us maintain a sense of self-respect and autonomy but also ensures that we are investing our time and energy in relationships that align with our values and aspirations.

In addressing toxic relationships, it is crucial to remember the principles discussed in the first chapter. By staying present and connected to our true essence, we can gain a deeper understanding of the dynamics at play in our relationships. Recognizing the patterns that cause suffering and acknowledging our role in perpetuating them allows us to take a step back and make more conscious decisions.

One powerful way to address toxicity in relationships is to become aware of our own thoughts and emotions without identifying with them. As we cultivate this awareness, we can observe the dynamics of our relationships without getting caught up in the drama. This conscious observation helps us to see the situation more objectively and allows us to take appropriate action from a place of clarity and understanding.

By embracing the practice of living in the present moment and connecting with our true selves, we can better identify and address toxic relationships. This empowers us to set boundaries, communicate our needs, and make the necessary changes to create healthier, more intentional relationships in our lives. Remember, living intentionally means taking responsibility for our own well-being and fostering relation- ships that align with our values and purpose.

When addressing these relationships, we often make mistakes that can exacerbate the situation and lead to further damage for both parties involved. It is crucial to approach these situations with mindfulness and Intentionalism to ensure that we can navigate through the toxicity without causing additional harm to ourselves or others.

One such mistake is reacting impulsively, letting emotions dictate actions. This response can lead to confrontations that escalate the situation, further damaging the relationship and causing emotional distress. Another misstep involves resorting to blaming and shaming in an attempt to address the toxicity. This approach rarely results in positive change, and it often pushes the other person further away, creating resentment and defensiveness. In some cases, people may choose to avoid addressing the problem altogether, hoping that it will resolve itself or simply disappear. Unfortunately, this passive approach can prolong the toxicity and prevent both parties from working through the issues and growing from the experience. It's essential to be mindful of these mistakes and strive for a more thoughtful approach when navigating toxic relationships.

Addressing these relationships with mindfulness and intention can empower us to make choices that align with our values, improve our relationships, or even remove them from our lives if necessary. We can use the same strategies we've discussed in previous chapters, such as staying mindful of our thoughts and emotions, living in the present moment, and making intentional choices.

Start by cultivating self-awareness to identify the patterns and dynamics in your toxic relationships. Observe your thoughts and emotions without judgment, recognizing how they might contribute to the toxicity. Acknowledge your role in perpetuating unhealthy patterns and be open to the possibility of change. Active listening is essential; focus on understanding the other person's perspective while avoiding interruptions or defensiveness. By being present and engaged in the conversation, you create a safe space for open and honest communication.

Establish clear boundaries to protect your well-being and maintain balance in your relationships. Communicate your needs and expectations calmly and assertively, enforcing those boundaries consistently. Embrace a growth mindset when working on your relationships, recognizing that both you and the other person have the potential to learn, change, and grow. Approach challenges with a positive attitude and remain open to learning from your experiences.

Cultivate empathy and compassion for the other person, understanding that they too may be struggling with their thoughts and emotions. This understanding can help create a more open and supportive environment for addressing the issues in the relationship. Take a step back and evaluate the relationship as a whole, considering whether it's worth the time and effort required to improve it. If the relationship continues to be toxic despite your efforts, it may be necessary to remove it from your life for your well-being.

If you're struggling to address toxic relationships on your own, consider seeking support from unbiased friends, family members, or a professional therapist. They can offer guidance, encouragement, and a fresh perspective on your situation. Mindfully and intentionally addressing toxic relationships can lead to healthier and more fulfilling connections. By being present, self-aware, and making conscious choices, you can take the necessary steps to improve or remove toxic relationships from your life. Don't forget that living intentionally means taking responsibility for your well-being and fostering relationships that align with your values and purpose.

Setting Boundaries

Setting boundaries is an essential aspect of cultivating healthy relationships and nurturing personal well-being. Establishing clear limits on what we are willing to accept from others, as well as the expectations we have for ourselves, enables us to maintain a sense of balance and harmony in our lives. By setting boundaries, we communicate our needs, desires, and values, ensuring that we are treated with respect and dignity. Furthermore, boundaries allow us to protect our mental and emotional well-being, providing a framework for self-care and fostering an environment in which we can thrive. Setting boundaries empowers us to create deeper, more fulfilling connections with others and a stronger sense of self. Here is a list of 10 steps for setting mindful and intentional boundaries.

1. Define personal boundaries: Clearly identify your physical, emotional, and mental limits to understand what you're comfortable with in various situations.
2. Assess past experiences: Reflect on past relationships and experiences to identify areas where boundaries were crossed or neglected and use these insights to inform your future boundary-setting.

3. Be specific and clear: When setting boundaries, be specific about what you need or expect from others to avoid confusion or misunderstandings.
4. Use assertive communication: Practice using "I" statements when discussing your boundaries to express your needs and feelings in a respectful, assertive manner.
5. Establish consequences: Clearly communicate the consequences if your boundaries are not respected and be prepared to follow through if necessary.
6. Start small: Begin by setting smaller, more manageable boundaries to build confidence and practice before addressing more significant or challenging issues.
7. Revisit and adjust boundaries as needed: Regularly review your boundaries to ensure they remain relevant and effective, making adjustments as needed to maintain healthy relationships.
8. Practice saying "no": Develop the ability to confidently say "no" when your boundaries are

at risk and avoid over-explaining or justifying your decision.
9. Model healthy boundaries: Demonstrate healthy boundary-setting in your own behavior, showing others how to respect and honor your limits.
10. Seek support when needed: If you're struggling to set or maintain boundaries, reach out to friends, family, or a professional therapist for guidance, encouragement, and assistance.

Reflection

In this chapter, we have explored the importance of cultivating supportive connections that align with our purpose and values, while addressing toxic relationships with mindfulness and care. Intentionalism is the driving force behind these efforts, as we strive to become true Intentionalists in all aspects of our lives. We have learned that being present in our relationships is crucial to fostering intentional connections. By recognizing that we are the creators of our thoughts and emotions, we become more empowered to shape our reality, taking ownership of our experiences and our interactions with others.

Through the practice of mindfulness, we can cultivate self-awareness, enabling us to recognize patterns and dynamics within our relationships that may not serve our intentions. By applying Carnegie's principles of under-standing, appreciation, and effective communication, we can develop stronger, more meaningful connections with others. Covey's emphasis on the importance of trust, respect, and cooperation further underscores the significance of nurturing intentional relationships in our lives.

Setting clear boundaries and addressing toxic relationships with compassion and empathy is essential for protecting our wellbeing and maintaining a sense of balance. In doing so, we open up the possibility of growth and transformation for both ourselves and the people we interact with. By adopting a growth mindset, we acknowledge that change is possible, and we create an environment in which we can thrive.

By embracing the principles of Intentionalism in this chapter, we can work towards building intentional relationships that support our personal growth and well-being. By being mindful of our thoughts, emotions, and actions, we take control of our reality, allowing us to create connections that not only enrich our own lives but also positively impact the lives of those around us. By living with intention, we naturally seek out relationships that are rooted in mutual respect, shared values, and genuine connection. These deep, meaningful bonds can significantly enhance our sense of belonging and contribute to our overall happiness and well-being.

Chapter 7: Nourishing Body & Mind

"A healthy outside starts from the inside." - Robert Urich

Self-care plays a pivotal role in maintaining our physical, emotional, and mental well-being. By prioritizing self-care, we not only create a strong foundation for personal growth and development but also ensure that we are better equipped to face the challenges that come our way with resilience and grace.

There are various techniques that can be incorporated into our daily lives, allowing us to effectively nourish our body and mind while remaining mindful of our thoughts, emotions, and actions. Mindfulness will serve as a cornerstone throughout this chapter, as it enables us to become more aware of our needs and to make conscious decisions that support our well-being.

Incorporating self-care into our daily routines is not a luxury but a necessity for achieving a harmonious, intentional life. By nourishing our body and mind, we not only foster a deeper connection with ourselves but also create a ripple effect that positively impacts our relationships, our work, and our overall sense of fulfillment.

The Importance of Self-care

In our fast-paced world, where we're often caught up in the whirlwind of responsibilities, expectations, and demands, it's easy to lose sight of what truly matters: taking care of ourselves. In the pursuit of happiness and personal growth, we can forget that the most essential aspect of intentional living is nurturing our own well-being.

Picture this: you're an adventurer embarking on a quest to discover the hidden treasure of intentional living. Along the way, you've equipped yourself with invaluable tools and knowledge gathered from an array of sources, including the profound wisdom of thought and spiritual leaders, the illuminating insights of spiritual enlightenment, and the transformative lessons in this very book. But as with any great adventure, the journey can be fraught with challenges, and there will be times when you feel weary, overwhelmed, or even lost. This is where the magic of self-care comes in!

Self-care, when practiced with mindfulness and intention, is like an elixir that rejuvenates your mind, body, and soul, allowing you to continue your quest with renewed energy, clarity, and focus. It's the compass that guides you back to your true north, reminding you of your purpose and empowering you to make choices that align with your values and goals.

As Intentionalists, we strive to create a life that is filled with meaning, purpose, and authenticity. By prioritizing self-care, we send a powerful message to ourselves and the world around us: "I matter. My well-being is important. I am worthy of love, care, and attention." When we nurture ourselves with the same care and compassion that we extend to others, we cultivate a deep sense of self-worth and inner strength.

Keep in mind, self-care and mindfulness are intimately intertwined. As we practice self-care, we're also honing our mindfulness skills, and becoming more attuned to our body's needs. This heightened awareness enables us to identify when we're feeling off-balance or depleted, empowering us to take proactive steps to nurture ourselves back to a state of equilibrium.

In essence, self-care is the lifeblood of intentional living. It's the nourishment that sustains us on our journey, the balm that heals our wounds, and the beacon of light that guides us through the darkest of times. By understanding the vital role self-care plays in our quest for a mindful and intentional life, we can unlock the door to a world where our well-being is not just an afterthought but the foundation upon which we build our dreams.

Unfortunately, some cultures prioritize external accomplishments over internal well-being, inadvertently neglecting the importance of nurturing our minds and emotions. It is crucial that we challenge this narrative and work towards normalizing mental health and self-care, both within our personal lives and our communities. By fostering open conversations about mental health, encouraging self-care practices, and creating supportive environments within our inner circles, we can help to shift societal attitudes and promote a healthier, more balanced way of living.

Nourishing the Mind

We often hear about the importance of taking care of physical health, but what about mental health? The mind is the powerhouse of our actions, emotions, and decisions. It deserves just as much attention and nourishment as our body.

Nourishing your mind means paying attention to and supporting your own mental well-being. It also means enhancing your brain function and protecting it from diseases that impair its normal functioning.

But how do you nourish your mind? There is no one-size-fits-all answer to this question. Rather, it's a complex recipe of many steps that all work together and complement each other.

Practice mindfulness. Mindfulness is an important practice to infuse more calm into your life. It means being aware of the present moment without judging it or wishing it was different. Mindfulness helps you reduce stress, improve focus, and regulate emotions.

You can practice mindfulness in many ways, such as meditation, breathing exercises, yoga, or simply paying attention to your senses. You can also use meditation apps such as Headspace or Simple Habit or even online courses to guide you through mindfulness practices. It doesn't have to take a lot of time or effort. Even a few minutes a day can make a difference in how you feel and think.

Reduce your screen time. There is an entire world beyond the internet. While technology can be useful and entertaining, it can also be addictive and distracting. Spending too much time on screens can affect your mood, sleep quality, attention span, and memory. To nourish your mind, try to limit your screen time and use it wisely. Set boundaries for yourself on when and how long you use your devices. Turn off notifications that are not essential or urgent. Avoid using screens before bed or first thing in the morning. Instead of scrolling through social media or watching videos endlessly, use your screen time for meaningful activities that enrich your mind. For example, you can read books or articles that interest you, learn something new, watch documentaries or educational videos, play games that challenge your brain, or connect with people who inspire you.

Quiet your thoughts. Quieting your mind is so important for reducing stress and anxiety. Our thoughts can be noisy and negative sometimes, making us feel overwhelmed or unhappy. Learning how to quiet them can help us gain more clarity, peace, and happiness. One way to quiet your thoughts is to write them down. Journaling can help you express yourself, process emotions, and gain insights. You don't have to follow any rules or format when journaling. Just write whatever comes to your mind without censoring yourself. Another way to quiet your thoughts is to practice gratitude. Gratitude can help you shift your focus from what's wrong to what's right in your life. It can also boost your mood, self-esteem, and optimism. You can practice gratitude by writing down three things you are grateful for every day, saying thank you more often, or expressing appreciation to others.

Make time for self-reflection: Self-reflection is the process of examining your thoughts, feelings, actions, and motivations. It helps you understand yourself better, learn from your experiences, and grow as a person.

Self-reflection is a nourishing practice that fosters personal growth in various ways. By engaging in self-reflection, you increase your self-awareness, becoming more conscious of your strengths, weaknesses, values, goals, and passions. This heightened awareness improves your decision-making, as it enables you to develop more clarity, confidence, and wisdom in making choices that align with your true self. Additionally, self-reflection enhances your creativity by tapping into your inner resources and unleashing new ideas, perspectives, and solutions.

Reflecting on yourself also strengthens your relationships, as it leads to more effective communication, deeper empathy, and more peaceful conflict resolution through a better understanding of yourself and others. You can practice self-reflection through various methods, such as asking yourself open-ended questions that challenge deep thinking, writing down your thoughts in a journal or notebook, or seeking feedback from others who know you well or have different perspectives. These practices help you gain new insights, perspectives, and advice that contribute to your personal growth and well-being.

The way you start your day can significantly influence your mood and productivity. A well-structured morning routine sets the tone for a positive, productive, and fulfilling day, while a poorly planned one can have the opposite effect. To nourish your mind in the morning, consider waking up early enough to give yourself sufficient time to prepare for the day without rushing or stressing.

Instead of immediately checking your phone or email, which can distract you from your priorities and expose you to negativity or stress, engage in an activity that makes you happy or energized. This could be listening to music, reading a book, playing with your pet, or pursuing a hobby.

Fueling your brain and body with a healthy breakfast is equally important. Choose foods rich in protein, fiber, healthy fats, antioxidants, and vitamins, and avoid those high in sugar, refined carbs, or artificial ingredients.

Lastly, take some time to plan your day and set realistic goals. This practice not only helps you organize your tasks and prioritize what's important, but also provides you with a sense of direction, purpose, and achievement that will carry you throughout the day.

Reading books is an excellent way to nourish your mind, as they can stimulate your imagination, expand your knowledge, improve your vocabulary, enhance your memory, and sharpen your critical thinking skills. Moreover, engaging in reading can reduce stress by helping you relax and escape from reality, subsequently lowering your blood pressure, heart rate, and cortisol levels.

Books can also boost your happiness by increasing empathy, compassion, and emotional intelligence while exposing you to positive messages, inspiring stories, and humor. Additionally, reading can ignite creativity by sparking new ideas, perspectives, and solutions through exposure to different genres, styles, and cultures. Furthermore, it promotes lifelong learning by keeping your mind active and curious, introducing you to new information, concepts, and skills.

You don't need to read an extensive amount to reap these benefits; even 15 minutes a day can make a difference. Choose any type of book that interests or challenges you and focus on enjoying the process and making reading a habit.

Learning something new is a fantastic yet simple way to nourish your mind. It can stimulate your brain, improve cognitive abilities, and boost self-confidence. Challenging yourself by stepping out of your comfort zone and overcoming obstacles through learning can promote growth, adaptability, and perseverance.

Additionally, acquiring new knowledge can offer a sense of accomplishment and satisfaction, positively impacting your mood, motivation, and self-esteem. It also creates connections with others who share your interests or goals, enhancing social skills, support networks, and overall happiness.

There are numerous ways to learn new things, such as taking online courses or workshops on topics that interest or benefit you, reading books or articles that teach new concepts or expand your horizons, and watching videos or listening to podcasts that educate and entertain. Engaging in games or puzzles that test logic, memory, or creativity, and trying new hobbies or activities that stimulate senses, skills, or passions are also effective ways to learn and grow.

Connecting with nature is one of the most powerful sources of nourishment for our minds. It can not only calm us down, but it can cheer us up and inspire us. Nature can even improve physical health through lowered blood pressure, a boosted immune system, and increased vitamin D levels.

Nature's soothing sounds, sights, smells, and sensations help reduce stress by allowing us to relax and unwind. The natural beauty, diversity, and wonder of the outdoors can boost our mood and make us feel happier and more positive. Moreover, nature's novel stimuli, patterns, and solutions can enhance creativity and innovative thinking.

Spending time in nature also promotes mindfulness and presence, offering opportunities to observe, appreciate, and explore the world around us. You don't need to venture far or devote significant time to reap these benefits. Simple activities such as taking a walk in the park or woods, sitting in the garden or on the balcony, planting flowers or herbs, watching the sunrise or sunset, or listening to birds or rain can help you connect with nature and nourish your mind.

Nourishing your mind is not only good for your mental health but also for your overall well-being. By following these tips, you can improve your brain function, reduce stress, increase happiness, and enhance creativity. It is not a one-time thing. It's an ongoing process that requires consistency and commitment. Make it a priority to nourish your mind every day, even if it's just for a few minutes. You not only need it. You deserve it.

Nourishing the Body

When it comes to intentional living, nourishing the body is just as important as nourishing the mind. What does it mean to nourish the body intentionally and mind- fully? It means making choices that prioritize our physical health and well-being and doing so with a sense of awareness and purpose by recognizing that our bodies are interconnected with our minds and emotions. The choices we make regarding our physical health can have a profound impact on our overall well-being.

Intentionally nourishing the body involves being mindful of what we put into it, from the foods we eat to the substances we consume. It means taking a holistic approach to health, considering not just what we eat, but also how we move, sleep, and manage stress. By being intentional in our choices and actions, we can cultivate a greater sense of physical wellness and vitality, which can in turn enhance our overall quality of life.

Nourishing the body intentionally and mindfully looks different for each individual, as we all have unique needs and preferences when it comes to our health. However, there are some key principles and practices that can help guide us toward a more intentional approach to physical well-being. Let's explore some of these principles and tips for incorporating intentional and mindful nourishment into our daily lives.

Eat mindfully. When it comes to nourishing your body, what you eat is just as important as how you eat. Take the time to savor each bite, chew slowly, and pay attention to how your body feels before, during, and after eating. This can help you develop a healthier relationship with food and make more intentional choices about what you put into your body.

Prioritize hydration. Staying hydrated is crucial for overall health and well-being. Make it a priority to drink plenty of water throughout the day and consider incorporating other hydrating beverages such as herbal tea or coconut water.

Move your body. Exercise is an important aspect of physical health, but it doesn't have to be a chore. Find activities that you enjoy and make them a regular part of your routine. Whether it's yoga, dancing, or hiking, moving your body in a way that feels good to you can be a form of self-care.

Practice self-care. Taking care of your body goes beyond just diet and exercise. Make time for self-care activities that help you feel relaxed and rejuvenated, such as taking a bath, getting a massage, or practicing meditation.

Get enough rest. Sleep is crucial for physical health, so make sure you're getting enough of it. Aim for 7-9 hours of sleep each night and consider developing a bedtime routine to help you wind down and prepare for restful sleep.

Breaking Through Barriers to Self-Care

Self-care is essential to our overall well-being, happiness, and personal growth. It encompasses a range of activities and practices designed to nurture our physical, emotional, and mental health. Despite its importance, many of us struggle to prioritize self-care in our daily lives due to various barriers. Let's explore the common obstacles that hinder our commitment to self-care and provide practical strategies for overcoming them, empowering us to lead a more balanced and fulfilling life.

Barrier 1: Time Constraints- One of the most common barriers to self-care is the perceived lack of time. Many people feel overwhelmed by their daily responsibilities, making it difficult to carve out time for themselves.

Strategies for overcoming time constraints:

- Schedule self-care activities: Treat self-care as an essential appointment by scheduling time for it in your calendar. This can help you prioritize self-care and hold yourself accountable.
- Break activities into smaller increments: If you struggle to find large blocks of time for self-care, try breaking activities into smaller increments. For example, instead of aiming for a 30-minute workout, try three 10-minute sessions throughout the day.
- Utilize pockets of downtime: Identify moments in your day when you have small pockets of downtime, such as during your commute or while waiting for appointments. Use these opportunities to engage in self-care activities, like deep breathing exercises or reading a book.

Barrier 2: Feelings of Guilt- Many individuals experience feelings of guilt when they prioritize self-care, often viewing it as indulgent or selfish. This guilt can be a significant barrier to incorporating self-care practices into daily life.

Strategies for overcoming feelings of guilt:

- Reframe self-care as essential: Remind yourself that self-care is not a luxury but a necessary component of maintaining your well-being. By prioritizing self-care, you are better equipped to care for others and fulfill your responsibilities.
- Develop a self-compassionate mindset: Cultivate self-compassion by recognizing that everyone deserves time for self-care, including you. Practice self-kindness and be gentle with yourself when you struggle to prioritize self-care.
- Surround yourself with supportive people: Connect with friends or family members who understand the importance of self-care and encourage you to prioritize your well-being. Their support can help alleviate feelings of guilt and reinforce the value of self-care.

Barrier 3: Prioritizing Others' Needs- Many people have a tendency to prioritize the needs of others over their own, often at the expense of their self-care. This can be particularly challenging for caregivers or those in helping professions.

Strategies for overcoming the tendency to prioritize others' needs:

- Establish boundaries: Clearly define and communicate your limits to others, and practice saying "no" when necessary. By setting boundaries, you protect your time and energy for self-care.
- Recognize the importance of self-care in caregiving: Understand that taking care of yourself is crucial for effectively caring for others. By prioritizing your own well-being, you can be more present and supportive of those who depend on you.
- Seek external support: Engage in support groups or therapy to help you navigate the challenges of balancing your needs with those of others. These resources can provide valuable insights, encouragement, and coping strategies.

Barrier 4: Lack of Awareness or Knowledge- Some people may not prioritize self-care simply because they are unaware of its importance or do not know how to effectively practice it.

Strategies for increasing awareness and knowledge:

- Educate yourself: Read books, and articles, or attend workshops on self-care to learn about its importance and various techniques. The more you know, the better equipped you will be to incorporate self-care into your life.
- Seek guidance from professionals: Consult with therapists, life coaches, or other professionals who can provide guidance and support on your self-care journey. They can help you develop a personalized self-care plan and offer expert advice on effective practices.
- Connect with like-minded individuals: Join online forums or local support groups where you can share experiences and learn from others who are committed to self-care. Surrounding yourself with a community of people who value self-care can help reinforce its

importance and provide inspiration for new practices.

Barrier 5: Financial Constraints- Financial limitations can be a barrier to self-care for some individuals, as certain activities may be perceived as too costly or unaffordable.

Strategies for overcoming financial constraints:

- Focus on low-cost or free self-care activities: There are numerous self- care practices that require little to no financial investment, such as going for a walk, practicing mindfulness meditation, or taking a relaxing bath. Explore these options and incorporate them into your self-care routine.
- Get creative with resources: Look for affordable or free resources in your community, such as local parks, libraries, or community centers that offer free workshops or classes.
- Prioritize self-care in your budget: If possible, allocate a portion of your budget to self-care activities that are important to you. This can

help reinforce the value of self-care and ensure you have the financial means to engage in the practices that bring you joy and support your well-being.

Reflection

The journey towards intentional living and mindfulness is one that requires us to be fully committed to nurturing our body, mind, and spirit. The practice of self-care is paramount in creating a strong foundation for personal growth and development. By prioritizing self-care, we empower ourselves to face life's challenges with resilience and grace, and we cultivate a greater sense of fulfillment in our daily lives.

Techniques such as mindfulness, meditation, physical exercise, and healthy eating, serve as tools that can be incorporated into our daily routines to effectively nourish our body and mind. By remaining mindful of our thoughts, emotions, and actions, we can become more attuned to our needs and make conscious decisions that support our well-being.

It is essential to acknowledge the common barriers that may hinder our commitment to self-care and to develop strategies that enable us to overcome them. By doing so, we can establish a more balanced, intentional lifestyle that aligns with our values and goals.

Self-care is not a luxury but a necessity for achieving a harmonious, purpose-driven life. By nourishing our body and mind, we not only foster a deeper connection with ourselves but also create a ripple effect that positively impacts our relationships, our work, and our overall sense of fulfillment.

Embracing self-care as a fundamental aspect of Intentionalism, allows us to cultivate a lifestyle that supports our well-being, happiness, and personal growth. This holistic approach to living empowers us to lead a more purposeful, balanced, and intentional life, one that aligns with our deepest desires, values, and aspirations.

As we conclude this chapter, let us commit to integrating self-care and mindfulness into our daily lives, continuously evolving and growing as we journey towards a more intentional, fulfilling existence.

Chapter 8: Overcoming Obstacles

"The greatest glory in living lies not in never falling, but in rising every time we fall." - Nelson Mandela

As the journey toward intentional living continues, inevitable obstacles will arise as we strive to lead a more purposeful and fulfilling life. Common obstacles to intentional living include physical and tangible things but also those that are created by our minds. By recognizing the power thoughts have in shaping reality, we can develop a deeper understanding of the internal and external challenges that may impede our progress.

Obstacles are an inherent part of the journey. Rather than viewing them as setbacks or insurmountable barriers, we can choose to reframe these challenges as opportunities for growth, self-discovery, and personal transformation. By doing so, we develop the resilience and adaptability necessary to persevere in our pursuit of a more intentional, fulfilling existence.

Common Obstacles and Strategies to Intentional Living

Start by acknowledging both external obstacles and those that exist within our minds. Understanding these barriers is crucial to our journey toward living with purpose and mindfulness. In this section, we will examine some of the common obstacles to intentional living and strategies to overcome them.

1. Procrastination and Indecision

Obstacle: One of the most pervasive obstacles to intentional living is procrastination and indecision. The tendency to put off important tasks or avoid making decisions can significantly impede our progress toward living a more purposeful life, as it prevents us from taking meaningful action and committing to our goals.

Strategy to overcome: Break tasks into smaller, manageable steps, which allows for better organization and efficiency. By setting deadlines and creating a schedule, you ensure that you stay on track and maintain a sense of structure. When faced with decisions, take the time to weigh the pros and cons of each option or seek advice from trusted sources.

2. Fear of Failure and Perfectionism

Obstacle: Fear of failure and perfectionism can also serve as significant barriers to intentional living. These fears can cause us to avoid taking risks, pursuing new opportunities, or embracing growth experiences. Additionally, perfectionism can lead to excessive self-criticism and unrealistic expectations, further hindering our progress toward living with purpose and intention.

Strategy to overcome: Embrace a growth mindset, viewing failure as a valuable opportunity to learn and grow. By focusing on progress rather than striving for perfection, you allow yourself the space to improve and evolve without the pressure of unrealistic expectations. Additionally, setting realistic goals and expectations will enable you to move forward on your journey with a sense of accomplishment, mitigating the effects of fear and perfectionism.

3. Lack of Clarity and Focus

Obstacle: A lack of clarity and focus can make it difficult to identify and prioritize our values, goals, and aspirations. Without a clear understanding of what we truly want, it becomes challenging to develop and maintain a meaningful sense of direction and purpose in our lives.

Strategy to overcome: Begin by setting clear, specific, and achievable goals that provide direction and purpose. Creating a personal mission statement or vision board can also help clarify your values and priorities, making it easier to concentrate on what truly matters. Moreover, regularly reviewing and adjusting your goals as needed ensures you remain adaptable and responsive to changing circumstances, allowing you to maintain a clear focus on your path toward personal growth and fulfillment.

4. Negative Thought Patterns and Limiting Beliefs

Obstacle: Our thoughts and beliefs play a powerful role in shaping our reality. Negative thought patterns and limiting beliefs can create significant obstacles to intentional living, as they often manifest in self-doubt, feelings of unworthiness, or the belief that we are incapable of achieving our goals.

Strategy to overcome: Practice mindfulness and self-awareness, enabling you to recognize and acknowledge these unproductive thoughts. Reframe limiting beliefs by focusing on your strengths and accomplishments, which helps shift your mindset towards a more empowering perspective. Additionally, cultivating a positive and supportive inner dialogue fosters a healthier self-image and encourages you to approach challenges with confidence, ultimately breaking free from the constraints of negative thinking.

5. Distractions and Overwhelm

Obstacle: In today's fast-paced, digitally connected world, distractions and overwhelm are increasingly common barriers to intentional living. The constant influx of information and demands on our attention can make it difficult to maintain focus, prioritize our goals, and cultivate mindful- ness in our daily lives.

Strategy to overcome: Prioritize tasks and set boundaries that minimize interruptions. Employing time management techniques, such as the Pomodoro Technique or time blocking, can help you stay focused and maintain productivity. Additionally, taking regular breaks and engaging in self-care activities are vital in preventing burnout, ensuring that you remain energized and capable of tackling your tasks effectively.

6. Resistance to Change

Obstacle: Embracing change and personal growth is a vital aspect of living intentionally, yet many people find it difficult to let go of familiar habits, routines, and comfort zones. This resistance can prevent us from pursuing new opportunities and experiences that align with our values and aspirations.

Strategy to overcome: Embrace change as an opportunity for growth and learning, rather than fearing or avoiding it. By cultivating a support system of friends, family, or mentors, you can gain valuable guidance and encouragement as you navigate the changes in your life. Moreover, practicing adaptability and resilience by facing challenges head-on will help you develop the necessary skills and mindset to not only cope with change but also thrive in the face of it.

7. Social Pressure and External Expectations

Obstacle: The influence of societal norms, family expectations, and peer pressure may cause us to prioritize the desires of others over our own or pursue goals that do not genuinely align with our values and passions.

Strategy to overcome: Clearly communicate your values and goals to others, ensuring they understand your priorities and intentions. Surround yourself with supportive and like-minded individuals who respect and encourage your pursuit of an authentic life. Additionally, learning to assertively say no to requests or situations that do not align with your values is crucial in maintaining your personal boundaries and staying true to your path.

8. Ego Identification

Obstacle: One of the most significant mental obstacles is the identification with the ego or the false sense of self. According to Tolle, the ego is a mental construct that consists of our thoughts, beliefs, and emotions, which we mistakenly believe to be our true selves. This identification with the ego can create a host of issues, including feelings of separation, competition, and judgment, ultimately hindering our ability to live intentionally and authentically.

Strategy to overcome: Practicing mindfulness and self-awareness, which allows you to recognize when you are identifying with your ego instead of your authentic self. Developing self-compassion and empathy towards yourself and others can help you let go of ego-driven behaviors and foster a more genuine connection with your inner self. Additionally, engaging in activities that cultivate a sense of interconnectedness, such as meditation or volunteering, can help you transcend the limitations of the ego and experience a deeper connection with others and the world around you.

9. The Pain-Body

Obstacle: The concept of the pain-body refers to the accumulation of unresolved emotional pain from our past experiences. The pain body can create significant obstacles to intentional living, as it often manifests in negative emotions and reactive patterns, preventing us from cultivating mindfulness and inner peace.

Strategy to overcome: Practicing mindfulness, which allows you to become more aware of the emotional pain you carry within. As you develop this awareness, you can then engage in emotional healing techniques to process and release these unresolved emotions. Such techniques might include therapy, journaling, or emotional release exercises, which can help you work through your pain body and gradually let go of the emotional baggage you have been carrying.

10. Attachment to the Past and Future

Obstacle: Another common mental obstacle is our attachment to the past and future, which Tolle refers to as the "time-bound mind." By constantly dwelling on past events or worrying about the future, we lose touch with the present moment – the only place where true intentional living can occur.

Strategy to overcome: Practicing mindfulness, which will help you remain present and focused on the current moment. This awareness can help you better appreciate and engage with the experiences you encounter. Additionally, learning to let go of past events through forgiveness and acceptance can free you from the burdens of regret or resentment, fostering a more balanced mindset. Lastly, cultivate a healthy relationship with the future by setting goals that align with your values while also practicing detachment. This approach allows you to work towards your aspirations without becoming overly fixated on specific outcomes.

11. Mind Chatter and Mental Noise

Obstacle: The constant stream of thoughts or "mind chatter" can create a significant barrier to intentional living. Tolle emphasizes that our inability to quiet the mind and find stillness within ourselves often leads to feelings of restlessness, anxiety, and discontent, ultimately preventing us from living in the present moment and aligning with our purpose.

Strategy to overcome: Engage in regular meditation or mindfulness practices, which can help cultivate mental stillness and reduce distractions. Creating a calming environment that supports focus and tranquility is another effective strategy, as it helps you stay centered and more resistant to external disruptions. Additionally, practice grounding techniques like deep breathing exercises or connecting with nature, which can bring you back to the present moment, fostering a sense of stability and inner peace. These combined approaches can help you effectively quiet mental noise and maintain a more focused and intentional mindset.

12. Resistance and Non-Acceptance

Obstacle: Resistance to the present moment and non-acceptance of our current reality can also create mental obstacles to intentional living. According to Tolle, resistance generates negative emotions and suffering, making it challenging to find peace, contentment, and clarity in our lives.

Strategy to overcome: Practicing mindfulness and self-awareness, which can help you recognize when you are experiencing resistance or struggling to accept reality. Cultivating gratitude and appreciation for the present moment is another effective strategy, as it allows you to focus on the positives and embrace your current circumstances. In addition, developing a problem-solving mindset can empower you to address challenges and obstacles head-on, rather than avoiding or resisting them.

13. The Illusion of Control

Obstacle: The illusion of control is the belief that we can control or manipulate external circumstances to create a desirable outcome. This illusion can lead to feelings of frustration, stress, and disappointment when reality does not align with our expectations, ultimately impeding our progress toward living with intention and mindfulness.

Strategy to overcome: Begin by practicing acceptance of situations and circumstances that are beyond your control. This will help you to let go of the need to exert control over every aspect of your life. Instead, shift your focus to what you can control, such as your actions, reactions, and mindset, which will empower you to make more intentional choices. Additionally, cultivating resilience is essential for dealing with uncertainty, so work on developing coping strategies that allow you to navigate life's unpredictable moments with grace and flexibility.

By recognizing and understanding these common obstacles to intentional living, we can develop a more compassionate and informed approach to our journey toward living with purpose and mindfulness. Acknowledging the power and influence of our thoughts, emotions, and external circumstances is a critical step in cultivating a more purposeful, mindful, and fulfilling existence.

By implementing these strategies, you will be better equipped to overcome obstacles and stay on track as you work towards cultivating a life of intentional living and mindfulness. Remember that personal growth is an ongoing process, and these strategies can be adapted and refined as you progress on your journey.

Building Resilience and Adaptability to Live the Life of Intentionalism

In our pursuit of intentional living, it is crucial to recognize that our journey will inevitably involve challenges, setbacks, and changes. Embracing resilience and adaptability is essential for navigating these complexities and maintaining a steadfast commitment to our goals, values, and aspirations. Let's explore the importance of resilience and adaptability in the context of intentional living, emphasizing the power of our minds, the need to accept what is, and the ability to create our reality simultaneously.

Resilience is the capacity to bounce back from adversity, setbacks, and challenges, while adaptability refers to our ability to adjust and respond effectively to change. Both resilience and adaptability are crucial qualities for intentional living, as they enable us to maintain our focus, purpose, and well-being amidst the unpredictability of life. The foundation of resilience and adaptability lies in our mindset. By cultivating mindfulness, we can become more aware of our thoughts and emotions, recognizing when they may be limiting our ability to adapt and respond effectively to challenges. Acceptance is also a key component of this mindset; by learning to accept the present moment and our current reality, we can reduce resistance and create a more conducive environment for growth and change.

One of the most effective ways to build resilience and adaptability is to view challenges and setbacks as opportunities for growth and learning. By adopting a growth mindset and actively seeking out new experiences, we can strengthen our capacity to adapt to change and overcome obstacles in our pursuit of intentional living. Emotional agility is the ability to recognize, understand, and manage our emotions effectively. By developing emotional agility, we can better navigate the ups and downs of life, maintain our focus on our goals and values, and cultivate a greater sense of inner peace and contentment.

Having a strong support system is essential for building resilience and adaptability. Supportive relationships provide encouragement, guidance, and resources that can help us overcome challenges and adapt to change. By surrounding ourselves with like-minded individuals who share our commitment to intentional living, we can foster a sense of connection and belonging that promotes resilience and adaptability.

Developing healthy routines and habits can also contribute to our resilience and adaptability. By prioritizing self-care, mind- fulness, and personal growth, we can create a strong foundation that enables us to maintain our well-being and focus amidst the inevitable challenges and changes we may encounter. Cultivating an attitude of gratitude and optimism can significantly impact our ability to build resilience and adaptability. By focusing on the positive aspects of our lives and expressing gratitude for our experiences, we can foster a more resilient and adaptable mindset that supports our journey toward intentional living.

Reflection

The journey towards intentional living invites us to confront the obstacles we face, transform our mindset, and cultivate resilience and adaptability in the face of life's challenges. Overcoming obstacles and embracing change are not merely external pursuits, but deeply rooted in the power of our minds and our ability to accept what is while actively creating our reality. The journey of acknowledging the common obstacles to intentional living, implementing effective strategies to overcome them, and fostering resilience and adaptability will not always be smooth. Unwavering commitment to intentional living, self-discovery, and growth will ultimately guide us in trans- forming not only ourselves but also the world around us.

Embrace the challenges, celebrate the victories, and know that the essence of intentional living lies in the continuous process of learning, evolving, and striving to become the best version of ourselves. As we accept what is and actively create our reality, we can navigate the complexities of life with greater ease, ultimately cultivating a more purposeful, mindful, and fulfilling existence.

Chapter 9: Living with Gratitude

"The more you practice gratitude, the more you see how much you have to be grateful for and your life becomes an ongoing celebration of joy and happiness." - Jack Canfield

Gratitude is more than just an expression of thankfulness; it is a powerful force that can transform our mental state, which, in turn, influences our external circumstances. By cultivating a deep sense of gratitude in our daily lives, we foster a profound connection with ourselves, others, and the world around us. This connection nurtures our well-being, fuels our resilience, and invites an abundance of joy and contentment into our lives.

Guided by the understanding that gratitude has the potential to reshape our mental state and, subsequently, our external reality, we will embark on a journey of self-discovery and growth, seeking to unlock the full potential of gratitude as a transformative force. Through this process, we will come to recognize the profound role gratitude plays in our pursuit of purpose, mindfulness, and fulfillment, as we cultivate a life enriched by the beauty of thankfulness, appreciation, and love.

Cultivating a Daily Sense of Gratitude

Cultivating a daily sense of gratitude involves a conscious shift in perspective, focusing on the positive aspects of our experiences and acknowledging the good in our lives.

Gratitude is a universal human feeling that transcends cultural boundaries and serves as a powerful tool for personal growth and transformation. By consciously recognizing and appreciating the positive aspects of our lives, we can shift our mindset from one of lack and discontent to one of abundance and satisfaction.

Gratitude can be seen as a practice, an attitude, and a way of life. Cultivating gratitude involves not only acknowledging the good things in our lives but also recognizing the sources of that goodness. These sources can range from tangible items such as our homes, possessions, and relationships to intangible experiences like our accomplishments, personal growth, and the beauty of nature.

To develop a consistent practice of gratitude, it is essential to be mindful and present in our daily lives. This involves being aware of our thoughts, emotions, and actions, as well as tuning into the world around us. By becoming more present, we can better appreciate the small moments of joy and beauty that often go unnoticed in the hustle and bustle of everyday life.

Gratitude is also closely connected to our relationships with others. By expressing our appreciation and acknowledging the kindness and support of those around us, we can strengthen our connections and foster a greater sense of belonging and community. This practice not only enhances our own well-being but also contributes to the well-being of those we interact with, creating a ripple effect of positivity and kindness.

Cultivating gratitude in daily life also involves embracing the concept of impermanence. By recognizing that everything in life is temporary and ever changing, we can develop a deeper appreciation for the present moment and the experiences that shape our lives. This understanding can help us to find gratitude even in the face of adversity and to see the silver linings in challenging situations.

Additionally, gratitude plays a key role in the development of self-compassion and self-acceptance. By acknowledging our strengths, accomplishments, and personal growth, we can foster a greater sense of self-worth and self-love. This practice enables us to be more gentle with ourselves, embrace our imperfections, and continue pursuing our goals and aspirations with determination and resilience. By consciously acknowledging the good in our lives, appreciating the sources of that goodness, and expressing our gratitude to others, we can foster a mindset of abundance, satisfaction, and contentment.

The Science Behind Gratitude

Gratitude is a powerful emotion that has been at the center of psychological research for decades. Numerous studies have shown that cultivating a sense of gratitude can have profound and lasting effects on our mental, emotional, and physical well-being. At its core, gratitude is an emotion that arises from recognizing and appreciating the positive aspects of our lives. From a psychological perspective, gratitude is closely related to the concepts of well-being, happiness, and life satisfaction. When we experience gratitude, our brain releases "feel-good" neurotransmitters, such as dopamine and serotonin, which contribute to positive emotions, enhance mood, and promote overall well-being.

Gratitude is also closely connected to the psychological concepts of cognitive appraisal and cognitive restructuring. Cognitive appraisal refers to the process by which we interpret and evaluate events and experiences. By focusing on the positive aspects of a situation, gratitude encourages a more favorable cognitive appraisal, which in turn can influence our emotional state and overall well-being. Cognitive restructuring, on the other hand, involves changing the way we think about events and experiences in order to promote a more positive and adaptive mindset. Gratitude supports cognitive restructuring by helping us reframe our thoughts and experiences in a more positive light.

Moreover, gratitude is closely related to the psychological concept of positive psychology, which emphasizes the study and cultivation of human strengths and virtues, such as gratitude, optimism, and resilience. Positive psychology encourages the pursuit of personal growth, happiness, and well-being, which aligns closely with the goals of intentional living.

The practice of gratitude has been shown to have significant effects on the brain. Neuroscientific research has revealed that gratitude activates various brain regions associated with emotional regulation, empathy, and social bonding. Some of the key brain regions involved in the experience of gratitude include the prefrontal cortex, the anterior cingulate cortex, and the hippocampus.

The prefrontal cortex, which is responsible for higher-order cognitive functions such as decision-making, planning, and emotional regulation, has been found to be more active during experiences of gratitude. This increased activation may contribute to the positive effects of gratitude on mental health and well-being.

The anterior cingulate cortex, which is involved in emotion processing and empathy, also shows increased activation during experiences of gratitude. This brain region plays a key role in the formation and maintenance of social bonds, suggesting that gratitude may help to strengthen our connections with others.

Finally, the hippocampus, a region critical for learning and memory, is also activated during experiences of gratitude. This activation may contribute to the long-term consolidation of positive experiences and emotions, which can ultimately support our mental health and well-being.

Cultivating a sense of gratitude in daily life is deeply rooted in psychological and neuroscientific principles. By understanding the psychological underpinnings of gratitude and embracing its transformative power, we can foster a sense of gratitude in our daily lives that not only enhances our well-being but also supports our journey toward intentional living. As we consciously choose to focus on the positive aspects of our lives, we create a ripple effect that influences our mental state, our relationships, and our external reality.

The Benefits of Gratitude

Gratitude is a powerful emotion that has been shown to profoundly impact our overall well-being. By cultivating an attitude of gratitude, we can enjoy a wide range of mental, emotional, and physical benefits. There are numerous ways that gratitude can affect overall well-being and be a simple yet transformative practice that enhances our lives.

Improved Mental Health: Gratitude has been linked to improved mental health, as it helps to reduce negative emotions such as envy, resentment, and frustration. By focusing on the positive aspects of our lives, we can experience greater happiness, life satisfaction, and emotional balance.

Increased Resilience: Cultivating gratitude can help us build resilience in the face of adversity. By maintaining a positive outlook and recognizing the good in our lives, even during difficult times, we can more effectively cope with stress and bounce back from setbacks.

Enhanced Physical Health: Gratitude has been shown to have positive effects on physical health as well.

Studies have found that individuals who practice gratitude regularly tend to have lower blood pressure, stronger immune systems, and better sleep quality. Grateful individuals also tend to engage in healthier habits, such as regular exercise and a balanced diet, which contribute to overall well-being.

Strengthened Relationships: Expressing gratitude can help to improve our relationships with others. By showing appreciation and recognizing the kindness and support of those around us, we can foster stronger connections, enhance trust, and promote feelings of belonging and togetherness.

Increased Empathy and Reduced Aggression: Gratitude has been linked to increased empathy, as it encourages us to recognize and appreciate the experiences and emotions of others. This heightened sense of empathy can lead to reduced aggression and increased compassion, promoting a more harmonious and understanding environment.

Greater Life Satisfaction: Individuals who regularly practice gratitude tend to have higher levels of life satisfaction. By focusing on the positive aspects of our lives and appreciating what we have, we can foster a greater sense of contentment, happiness, and fulfillment.

Heightened Mindfulness and Presence: Gratitude encourages us to be more mindful and present in our daily lives. By appreciating the present moment and recognizing the beauty in everyday experiences, we can cultivate a deeper connection to ourselves and the world around us.

Improved Self-Esteem and Confidence: Gratitude can have a positive impact on our self-esteem and confidence. By appreciating our achievements, strengths, and personal growth, we can foster a greater sense of self-worth and self-compassion, empowering us to continue pursuing our goals and aspirations.

Incorporating gratitude into our daily lives can yield numerous benefits for our overall well-being, encompassing mental, emotional, and physical health.

Practicing Gratitude

Integrating gratitude practices into our daily routines can greatly enhance our intentional living journey, as it helps us to cultivate a positive mindset, strengthen our connections, and foster personal growth. In this section, we will explore 6 gratitude practices that can be incorporated into our lives to support intentional living and overall well-being.

1. Gratitude Journaling:

One of the most effective ways to practice gratitude is by keeping a gratitude journal. Set aside time each day to write down a few things you are grateful for, focusing on both the small, everyday moments and the larger, more significant experiences. This practice encourages you to become more aware of the positive aspects of your life and can help to rewire your brain to focus on the good rather than the negative.

2. Gratitude Meditation:

This involves focusing your attention on feelings of thankfulness and appreciation while in a meditative state. This practice can help to deepen your sense of gratitude, reduce stress, and promote a greater connection to the present moment. To practice gratitude meditation, find a quiet space, close your eyes, and take a few deep breaths. Then, bring to mind several things for which you are grateful and allow yourself to fully experience the emotions associated with this gratitude.

3. Gratitude Letters or Emails:

Writing letters or emails expressing gratitude to the people in your life can be a powerful way to strengthen relationships and acknowledge the kindness and support of others. Set aside time to write heartfelt messages to friends, family members, or colleagues, detailing the specific reasons you are grateful for them and the impact they have had on your life.

4. Gratitude Affirmations:

These are positive statements that help to cultivate a grateful mindset. By repeating these affirmations regularly, you can shift your focus from negative thoughts and experiences to the positive aspects of your life. Some examples of gratitude affirmations include:

"I am grateful for the love and support of my friends and family."

"I appreciate the opportunities that come my way and the lessons they teach me."

"I am thankful for the beauty and abundance that surrounds me."

5. Gratitude Walks:

Incorporating gratitude into your daily walks or outdoor activities can help you to become more present and appreciative of the world around you. As you walk, take the time to notice and appreciate the beauty in your surroundings, from the warmth of the sun to the sound of birdsong or the colors of the changing seasons.

6. Mindful Gratitude Practices:

Incorporating gratitude into daily routines, such as expressing thanks before meals or reflecting on the positive aspects of your day before bedtime, can help to promote a more grateful mindset and increase well-being. By making gratitude a consistent part of your daily life, you can foster a greater connection to the present moment and enhance your intentional living journey.

Reflection

Living with gratitude is a powerful and transformative practice that serves as a cornerstone of intentional living. Through the cultivation of gratitude in our daily lives, we can positively impact our mental, emotional, and physical well-being, as well as create a ripple effect that influences our relationships, our work, and our overall sense of fulfillment.

By consciously choosing to focus on the positive aspects of our lives and adopting a grateful mindset, we can overcome the obstacles that may arise on our path and create a life that is more mindful and fulfilling. In the pursuit of intentional living, always remember to cherish the moments of joy, love, and contentment that we encounter along the way. By doing so, we not only nourish our own well-being but also contribute to the well-being of those around us, ultimately creating a more harmonious, compassionate, and intentional world.

Chapter 10: Finding Purpose & Fulfillment

"The two most important days in your life are the day you are born and the day you find out why." - Mark Twain

As we embark on the final chapter of our exploration into intentional living, we arrive at the heart of the matter: finding purpose and fulfillment. Our lives are a complex tapestry of experiences, relationships, and personal growth. At the core of this intricate weave lies our purpose – the driving force that propels us forward and gives meaning to our existence. Uncovering our purpose is essential to living an intentional life, as it allows us to align our actions with our values.

Life is a journey of self-discovery and on that journey, our purpose becomes clear as we seek to understand the essence of what it means to live a life that is not only meaningful but also deeply fulfilling. By living with conscious intention, we not only create a strong foundation for personal growth and development but also cultivate a mindful awareness that allows us to navigate the complexities of life with grace, resilience, and inner peace.

With each mindful step we take, we can shape our lives into a reflection of our innermost desires, ultimately creating a world that resonates with our values, passions, and aspirations.

Discovering Your Purpose in Life: The Cornerstone of Intentionalism

The journey of discovering one's purpose in life is a deeply personal and transformative experience. It represents an essential aspect of living with intention, guiding our choices, actions, and decisions in a way that resonates with our deepest values and desires.

Intentionalism is centered around the idea of living our lives with conscious awareness, deliberate choices, and purposeful actions. The process of discovering our purpose serves as a foundation for this way of living, providing us with a clear sense of direction and meaning. Purpose acts as a compass, helping us navigate the complexities of our lives and ensuring that our actions align with our core beliefs and aspirations. When we are aware of our purpose, we are better equipped to make decisions that resonate with our deepest values, promoting a sense of coherence and congruence in our lives. This sense of alignment fosters a greater connection to ourselves and others.

Discovering our purpose in life not only provides us with direction but also serves as a catalyst for personal growth and development. As we pursue our purpose, we are often challenged to stretch beyond our comfort zones, confront our fears, and embrace our vulnerabilities. This process of self-discovery and growth is an integral part of intentional living, allowing us to evolve and adapt in the face of change and uncertainty. Our sense of purpose is intricately connected to the bigger picture of our lives, encompassing relationships, work, and personal aspirations. Ultimately, discovering purpose in life is a fundamental aspect of intentional living. It provides us with a clear sense of direction, fosters personal growth and development, and helps us understand our place within the larger context of our lives.

Strategies for Finding Purpose

Discovering your purpose is a deeply personal journey that can be approached from various angles. While everyone's path to finding their purpose may be unique, there are common sources and strategies that can provide guidance and inspiration in this process. Reflect on your values and principles as discussed in Chapter 3. One of the most effective ways to begin uncovering your purpose is to dive into your core values and passions. What is truly important to you? What activities or pursuits make you feel alive and energized? By reflecting on your values and interests, you can gain insights into the aspects of life that hold the most meaning for you. This process can help you identify patterns and themes that point toward your deeper purpose, providing you with a clearer sense of direction and motivation.

Explore Spiritual Teachings and Beliefs. For many individuals, spiritual teachings and beliefs serve as a powerful source of guidance and inspiration in the quest for purpose. Religion, philosophy, and other spiritual traditions can provide frameworks for understanding our place in the world and our ultimate purpose. By engaging with these teachings, you can gain insights into the broader context of your life and the underlying principles that guide your actions and decisions. This exploration can help you clarify your purpose and align it with your spiritual beliefs and values.

Seek the Wisdom of Others. Engaging in conversations with mentors, loved ones, or spiritual leaders can provide you with valuable insights and perspectives to help you better understand your purpose. These individuals can act as sounding boards, offering guidance, encouragement, and support as you navigate the complexities of self-discovery.

Observe Your Natural Talents and Skills. By identifying areas in which you excel or feel a sense of ease and flow, you can begin to understand how your unique gifts can be channeled toward a greater purpose. Reflect on the activities and pursuits that come naturally to you and consider how they might align with your values, passions, and sense of purpose.

Embrace the Journey of Self-Discovery. It requires patience, openness, and a willingness to explore the depths of your being. Remember that your purpose may evolve and shift over time, reflecting your growth and development as an individual. Embrace this process of exploration and transformation, trusting that your purpose will reveal itself as you continue to live with intention and conscious awareness.

What is my purpose?

"The purpose of our lives is to be happy." - Dalai Lama

My beliefs are deeply ingrained in a profound scripture verse that eloquently states, "...men are, that they might have joy." This simple yet powerful declaration has significantly influenced my understanding of life's purpose and the role that joy plays in our existence. It conveys the idea that all individuals are here on Earth to experience joy in every regard, both externally and internally, making it a fundamental aspect of our lives.

As Tolle teaches, my true essence is Joy; this concept reinforces the notion that not only do I embody joy, but I am also meant to embrace it wholeheartedly in its various forms. Whether it be through personal growth, the pursuit of my passions, or the relationships I cultivate, the pursuit of joy serves as a guiding force in my life.

The teachings of Jesus Christ further emphasize the importance of joy by encouraging us to help others find this sublime state of being, which is intrinsically linked to the pure love of Christ. By extending our compassion, understanding, and support to those around us, we not only experience joy ourselves but also become instruments in bringing it into the lives of others.

In essence, my life's purpose is to be and find joy in all its manifestations and to share this gift with others. By assisting others in their journey to uncover and experience the profound joy that life offers, we create a ripple effect that radiates outward, ultimately leading us all to Christ Himself. Through this journey, we are reminded of the interconnectedness of our experiences and the importance of fostering a world where joy, love, and compassion reign supreme.

What is Your Purpose?

A part of me wishes I could just tell you that answer. Still, the larger part of me knows that finding one's purpose is a deeply personal and transformative journey that requires introspection, self-discovery, and genuine exploration of one's values, passions, and beliefs. You must find this understanding of your purpose yourself. My hope is that throughout this book you would have found the tools to begin to dive into your heart and start to understand your purpose. If not and you are still searching to uncover your unique purpose, here are some more steps to guide you along the way:

1. Reflect on your values: Consider the principles and values that are most important to you. What do you stand for? What drives your actions and decisions? Identifying your core values can serve as a compass, helping you navigate life's challenges and align your actions with your purpose.

2. Explore your passions: What activities or pursuits bring you joy and fulfillment? Consider the hobbies, interests, and causes that deeply resonate with you. These passions can provide valuable insights into your purpose and the path you should follow.
3. Examine your strengths and talents: Reflect on the unique strengths and talents that you possess. What are you naturally good at? What skills have you developed over time? Recognizing your innate abilities can offer guidance on the ways in which you can contribute to the world and fulfill your purpose.
4. Seek inspiration in spiritual teachings and beliefs: Delve into spiritual texts, religious teachings, or philosophies that resonate with you. These sources of wisdom can offer valuable insights and guidance in uncovering your life's purpose.
5. Look for patterns in your life: Reflect on the recurring themes, experiences, and lessons that have shaped your life. Are there any common threads that link these events together?

Identifying patterns can help you gain clarity on your purpose and the lessons you are meant to learn.

6. Set meaningful goals: Establish personal and professional goals that align with your values, passions, and strengths. These goals should be driven by your desire to live a purposeful life and contribute positively to the world around you.

7. Seek support and guidance: Reach out to mentors, friends, or family members who can offer valuable insights and advice as you embark on your journey to find your purpose. Their perspectives may help you uncover new possibilities and gain clarity on your path.

8. Practice mindfulness and self-awareness: Cultivate a daily practice of mindfulness, meditation, or introspection to help you stay connected with your inner self and maintain a clear vision of your purpose.

9. Be patient and persistent: Finding your purpose is a journey that unfolds over time. Embrace the process and remain open to new

experiences, lessons, and opportunities that come your way. Remember that your purpose may evolve as you grow and change.

By taking the time to explore your values, passions, strengths, and beliefs, you will gradually uncover your unique purpose. Trust the process and remember that living a life of intention and meaning is the key to unlocking your true potential and experiencing lasting fulfillment.

Living in Harmony with Your Purpose

In the pursuit of a life filled with meaning and fulfillment, aligning your actions with your purpose is of paramount importance. When your actions are in harmony with your purpose, you create a powerful synergy. Living in alignment with your purpose generates a sense of coherence and consistency in your life. This sense of coherence allows you to navigate life with greater clarity, direction, and focus.

Aligning your actions with your purpose fosters a strong sense of authenticity and integrity. By acting in accordance with your values and passions, you are better able to remain true to yourself and cultivate a life that is genuinely reflective of who you are. This authenticity bolsters your self-esteem and self-confidence, empowering you to make bolder decisions and take calculated risks in pursuit of your dreams.

Living in harmony with your purpose can significantly enhance your emotional well-being. Engaging in activities that align with your purpose provides a deep sense of satisfaction and fulfillment, leading to increased levels of happiness and contentment. Furthermore, when your actions are in sync with your purpose, you are more likely to experience positive emotions, such as joy, gratitude, and love, which contribute to your overall mental health and well-being. When you are deeply connected to your purpose, you are better equipped to navigate life's inevitable challenges and setbacks. This connection provides you with the inner strength and determination necessary to persevere and overcome obstacles, ultimately contributing to your personal growth and development.

By pursuing a life guided by your values and passions, you naturally attract like-minded individuals who share similar beliefs and aspirations. These meaningful connections can provide you with a strong support network, fostering a sense of belonging and enhancing your overall quality of life. You also become a powerful force for good, inspiring others to live more intentional, purpose-driven lives. This collective impact has the potential to create lasting, meaningful change on a global scale.

This alignment of actions with purpose fosters a sense of coherence, authenticity, emotional well-being, resilience, and social connectedness while also contributing positively to the lives of others and the world at large.

The Power of Conscious Choices and Actions

Through consistently reflecting on values, desires, and aspirations, we cultivate a deeper understanding of who we are and what truly matters to us. This increased self-awareness allows us to make more informed decisions, enabling us to prioritize time and energy on activities that genuinely align with core beliefs. When we take charge of our lives by making deliberate choices and engaging in purposeful actions, we assert control over our destinies. This sense of autonomy enables us to navigate life with greater confidence and conviction, ultimately leading to a more satisfying and self-determined existence.

When approaching life with intention, we naturally become more attuned to the present moment, fostering a deeper connection to ourselves, others, and our surroundings. This mindful awareness can significantly enhance our emotional well- being, as it allows us to savor positive experiences, cope more effectively with challenges, and foster a more profound appreciation for the beauty and richness of life.

Living a life of Intentionalism can contribute to the development of healthier and more balanced lifestyles. When we approach life with a clear sense of purpose and commitment to our values, we are more likely to engage in activities that challenge us, broaden our horizons, and contribute to our personal development. This ongoing process of growth and self-discovery can be deeply rewarding, fostering a greater sense of meaning and satisfaction in our lives.

Lastly, Intentionalism can have a profound impact on our relationships and social connections. By living with intention, we naturally seek out relationships that are rooted in mutual respect, shared values, and genuine connection. These deep, meaningful bonds can significantly enhance our sense of belonging and contribute to our overall happiness and well-being.

Living a more fulfilling life through Intentionalism involves cultivating a heightened sense of self-awareness, autonomy, mindfulness, balance, personal growth, and meaningful relationships. By embracing the power of conscious choices and deliberate actions, we can create a life that not only aligns with our values and passions but also fosters a profound sense of meaning, satisfaction, and overall well-being.

Reflection

Embodying the essence of joy within ourselves, we are called to both experience and radiate this divine gift. Our purpose, intricately woven into the fabric of our existence, is to embrace the joy that lies at our core and extend it to others, thereby manifesting the pure love of Christ in our lives and the world around us.

By discovering our unique purpose, aligning our actions with it, and embracing the principles of Intentionalism, we pave the way for a more meaningful, satisfying, and joyful existence. As we've discussed my purpose, rooted in the pursuit of joy and assisting others in finding their own joy, it is crucial to remember that each individual's purpose is unique and holds the potential to guide their life towards extraordinary heights.

By embarking on this quest for purpose and fulfillment, we not only enrich our own lives but also positively impact the lives of those around us, fostering a sense of interconnectedness and shared humanity. As we strive to live intentionally and purposefully, we create a ripple effect that extends far beyond our immediate circles, ultimately contributing to the collective well-being and happiness of our world. Let us embrace our unique purposes with open hearts and open minds, empowering ourselves and others to lead lives filled with intention, meaning, and fulfillment.

Chapter 11: Maintaining Intentionalism

"The secret of change is to focus all your energy, not on fighting the old, but on building the new." - Socrates

As we journey through the realm of intentional living, we now arrive at a crucial juncture—maintaining the practices and principles that we've learned, thus ensuring the sustainability of a purposeful, mindful, and fulfilling life. While discovering and implementing the tenets of intentional living is a vital first step, fostering the commitment and perseverance to continue along this path is equally essential. Let's now jump into the art of maintaining intentional living over time and provide guidance on how to remain steadfast in our pursuit of a more meaningful and connected existence.

Let's analyze various strategies for sustaining intentional living, understanding that the path to purposeful living is a dynamic and evolving journey. By developing the ability to adapt, grow, and learn from our experiences, we can continue to refine our approach and maintain a consistent connection to our purpose and values.

Building accountability and support systems is an integral part of maintaining our commitment to intentional living. In this chapter, we will discuss the importance of surrounding ourselves with like-minded individuals, creating supportive communities, and cultivating a network that encourages us to remain true to our intentions and aspirations.

Lastly, we will embark on a journey of reflection, examining the impact of intentional living on our overall life satisfaction. Through this introspection, we will gain a deeper understanding of how our commitment to living with intention has transformed our lives, both internally and externally. By recognizing the tangible benefits of intentional living, we can reinforce our motivation to continue on this path, ultimately nurturing a more fulfilling, purpose-driven existence.

With each step we take, the practices and principles of intentional living become more deeply ingrained in our lives. As we move forward, let us embrace the challenge of maintaining intentional living with open hearts and open minds, knowing that our unwavering dedication to this journey will lead us to a more meaningful, connected, and joyful life.

Strategies to Maintain Intentional Living

As we venture deeper into the world of intentional living, it becomes crucial to develop and implement effective strategies for maintaining this approach over time. Life presents us with a plethora of challenges and distractions, but with the right tools and techniques, we can stay steadfast in our pursuit of a purpose-driven and fulfilling life.

Sustaining a purposeful and mindful lifestyle requires adopting various strategies that help maintain your commitment and encourage personal growth. One way to stay focused on your journey is by celebrating small victories. Acknowledging and appreciating these moments nurtures a sense of achievement and boosts motivation. Continual learning is another essential aspect, as dedicating time to exploring new ideas, perspectives, and approaches enriches your experience and enables you to adapt and grow.

Conducting regular life audits can help you assess different areas of your life, such as relationships, career, and personal growth. This practice allows you to identify where you may have veered off course and realign your actions with your core values. Setting and enforcing personal boundaries is equally important, as it protects your time, energy, and well-being, helping you maintain balance and stay true to your principles.

Engaging in creative outlets, such as writing, painting, or music, offers a way to express your thoughts, emotions, and aspirations, reinforcing your commitment to a meaningful life. Coupled with a growth mindset, embracing the belief that you can learn and improve from your experiences, you can view challenges as opportunities for personal development.

Utilizing technology mindfully can also support your journey. Harness digital tools like productivity apps and online communities to enhance your efforts, while remaining aware of screen time and its potential impact on your well-being. Finally, create a personal mantra or affirmation that encapsulates your commitment to living with purpose. Regularly repeating this phrase serves as a reminder of your values and goals, helping you recenter yourself when faced with distractions or setbacks. By employing these strategies, you can foster a sustainable approach to living a meaningful life that supports your personal growth and well-being.

By incorporating these new strategies into your daily life, you can maintain and strengthen your commitment to intentional living over time. As you navigate the challenges and opportunities that life presents, these approaches will help you stay true to your purpose and values, ultimately fostering a more fulfilling and intentional existence.

Building Support Systems

Having support systems to be held accountable is crucial for maintaining your intentional living journey. These systems help to keep you on track, provide encouragement during difficult times, and offer guidance and resources to overcome obstacles. Here are 8 ways to build and sustain effective support systems for holding yourself accountable to promote a more intentional lifestyle.

1. **Leverage personal relationships**

    Share your intentions and goals with close friends, family members, or a trusted mentor. By discussing your aspirations and the steps you're taking to live more intentionally, you create a support network that can hold you accountable, offer advice, and celebrate your achievements.

2. **Create or join a group**

    Connect with like-minded individuals who share your commitment to intentional living. This could be a local group or an online community. Participating in a group provides a space to exchange ideas, share experiences, and learn from others who are on a similar journey.

3. **Set measurable goals**

    Break down your intentional living objectives into smaller, measurable goals. Tracking your progress and celebrating milestones can help you stay accountable and motivated. Be flexible and adapt your goals as needed to maintain momentum and align with your evolving intentions.

4. **Establish routines and rituals**

    Incorporate intentional living practices into your daily routines and rituals. Consistency is key for maintaining momentum, and embedding these habits into your daily life can help you stay focused on your long-term objectives.

5. **Use a journal or planner**

    Documenting your progress, thoughts, and reflections in a journal or planner can be an effective way to maintain accountability. Regularly review your entries to assess your growth, identify areas for improvement, and celebrate your accomplishments.

6. **Seek professional guidance**

    Engage with professionals, such as life coaches, therapists, or spiritual advisors, who can offer guidance, support, and resources tailored to your unique needs and goals. These experts can provide valuable insights and help you navigate challenges along your intentional living journey.

7. Utilize digital tools and resources

Leverage technology to stay accountable and track your progress. Apps, websites, and online courses can provide valuable resources to support your intentional living journey, while also offering a platform to connect with others for encouragement and inspiration.

8. Practice self-compassion

Remember to be kind to yourself during your intentional living journey. Acknowledge that setbacks and challenges are a natural part of the process and use them as opportunities for growth and learning. Self-compassion can help you maintain motivation and resilience in the face of obstacles.

Building and nurturing support systems is vital for sustaining your commitment to intentional living and makes it much easier to be held accountable. As you develop and strengthen these systems, you'll find that they not only help you stay on track but also enrich your journey, providing opportunities for growth, connection, and self-discovery.

The Impact of Intentionalism

Intentional living has the power to significantly shape and elevate overall satisfaction in life. By mindfully making choices and engaging in actions that align with your values, goals, and purpose, you pave the way for a more meaningful and fulfilling existence.

One profound effect of intentional living is the enhancement of self-awareness. As you embark on this journey, you'll find that introspection and self-discovery come naturally, allowing you to better understand your values, strengths, and aspirations. This increased self-awareness leads to more authentic choices, which, in turn, contribute to a greater sense of fulfillment and satisfaction in life.

Intentional living enables you to clarify and prioritize your values, which in turn fosters a sense of purpose and direction. By setting goals aligned with your true self, you create a more gratifying life experience.

This mindful approach to life also encourages the cultivation of deeper, more meaningful connections with others. By consciously investing time and energy in relationships that align with your values, you create a support network that enriches your life and contributes to your overall happiness.

Resilience is another key aspect that intentional living promotes, as it better equips you to navigate challenges and setbacks. Learning to adapt and grow through adversity ultimately contributes to overall satisfaction.

Furthermore, embracing mindfulness and presence allows you to engage more fully in each moment. This heightened sense of engagement enhances our appreciation for life's experiences, leading to a more joyful existence.

Lastly, your commitment to living with purpose may inspire and positively influence those around you. The knowledge that your actions have a meaningful impact on others contributes to a greater sense of satisfaction and purpose, enriching your life and the lives of those around you.

By taking the time to reflect on the ways intentional living has enhanced your life satisfaction, you not only deepen your understanding of its benefits but also cultivate gratitude for the transformative power of living with purpose and intention. This gratitude serves to reinforce your commitment to intentional living, propelling you forward on your journey to a more meaningful and fulfilling life.

In closing, the journey of discovering purpose, aligning actions with that purpose, and living a more fulfilling life through intentionalism is a transformative and powerful endeavor that offers endless opportunities for growth and self-discovery. As we have explored, the process of understanding your purpose and aligning your life with it paves the way for a deeper sense of fulfillment, satisfaction, and overall well- being. Intentional living is not only about identifying what truly matters to you but also about taking consistent action to manifest those values and aspirations in your everyday life, ultimately creating a harmonious and meaningful existence.

Embrace this journey with curiosity, compassion, and determination, and you will find yourself living a life that is not only purposeful but also profoundly enriching and gratifying. Along the way, you will uncover new insights about yourself, your relationships, and your place in the world, which will only serve to further deepen your sense of purpose and direction.

Let us not forget, the pursuit of intentional living is an ongoing process, one that requires continuous reflection, adaptation, and growth. It is a lifelong commitment to personal evolution and self-improvement, guided by your deepest desires and highest potential. Be patient with yourself as you navigate this path, and know that every step you take, no matter how small, brings you closer to the life you envision.

As you continue on this journey, surround yourself with supportive and like-minded individuals who share your passion for intentional living. These connections will serve as a powerful source of inspiration, motivation, and encouragement, propelling you forward on your path toward a more fulfilling and purpose-driven life.

Embark on this incredible adventure with an open heart and an open mind, trusting in the transformative power of intentional living to shape your life in profound and meaningful ways. Let the knowledge that you are consciously creating a life aligned with your purpose be a source of strength and motivation, propelling you forward into a future filled with joy, fulfillment, and a deep sense of personal satisfaction.

Chapter 12: Concluding Thoughts

Let us take a moment to reflect on the incredible insights and practical strategies we have uncovered throughout our exploration of intentional living. My hope is that this book has provided a roadmap for cultivating a life that is not only meaningful and fulfilling but also deeply connected to our true essence and purpose.

As we now pause to reflect on our personal growth and development, it is important to recognize and appreciate the progress we have made on this journey of self-discovery. Each step we have taken and each moment of insight we have experienced have contributed to our evolution as individuals and have brought us closer to the life we aspire to live.

Intentional living is not a destination but rather an ongoing process of growth and self-improvement. It is a commitment to living our lives with purpose, authenticity, and mindfulness, constantly refining our vision and adjusting our actions to reflect our deepest values and desires.

Embrace the power of the present moment, as it is the gateway to a life lived with intention, purpose, and the boundless joy that comes from aligning with our true essence.

As we reach the end of our journey together, I would like to leave you with some final words of encouragement and inspiration. Change can be challenging, but it is essential for growth and progress. As you move forward, remember that every step you take, no matter how small, is a step in the right direction. It takes courage and determination to challenge old patterns and embrace new ways of thinking and living, but the rewards are well worth the effort.

Intentionalism lies at the heart of this transformation. By focusing on your values, purpose, and the present moment, you can make deliberate choices that align with your highest aspirations. Intentionalism empowers you to create a life that reflects your true essence, fostering deep connections with yourself, others, and the world around you.

If there is one key takeaway that I hope will resonate with you, it is the power of living in the present moment. Now is the only time that truly exists, and it is the only place where we have the power to make a difference. By embracing the present and focusing our energy and attention on what we can control, we can create a more intentional, purposeful, and fulfilling life.

As you navigate the complexities of life and face inevitable challenges, remember to return to the present moment, again and again. By grounding yourself in the Now, you can tap into your inner strength, resilience, wisdom, and ultimately harness the power to shape your own destiny.

In closing, I invite you to take a deep breath, let go of any lingering doubts or fears, and commit to embarking on this transformative journey toward becoming an Intentionalist. You have the power within you to create a life of intention, purpose, and joy. Stay curious and open to new experiences, welcome the challenges that life presents, and celebrate your accomplishments along the way. Embrace the present moment and allow it to guide and inspire you as you step boldly into your future.

As you continue your journey, remember that you are never alone. There is an entire community of like-minded individuals who share your desire to live with intention and purpose. Seek out these connections and support one another in our collective pursuit of a more fulfilling life.

Together, we can create a world that is more intentional, more compassionate, and more deeply connected to what truly matters. Embrace the power of the present moment, trust your inner compass and allow it to illuminate your path toward your highest potential and your most authentic self. In doing so, you will find the joy, purpose, and fulfillment you seek as a true Intentionalist.

Special Thanks

I would like to express my gratitude to the people who have played a significant role in shaping who I am today and for showing me the best way to be who I truly am.

I want to express my deepest love and appreciation to my beautiful, amazing wife, Miranda. Thank you for your endless support and for patiently listening to my endless streams of thoughts, even when I start babbling on. Your love, understanding, and companionship have been my pillars of strength, and I am forever grateful to have you by my side. I love you, now and always.

To my loving parents, thank you for raising me with such care and dedication. Your long, late-night talks have not only guided me through life but have also inspired my journey to intentional living. Your unwavering support and love mean the world to me.

To my siblings, thank you for the irreplaceable bond we share and for the countless memories we've created together. Your love, laughter, and support have played an essential role in my growth, and I am forever grateful for the strong foundation we've built as a family.

I would also like to extend my heartfelt appreciation to my best bud, Dallin. Thank you for always having my back and helping me see things from different perspectives. Your insights have enriched my thinking, and I am grateful for our open and sincere friendship.

Last but certainly not least, to you, my readers and friends, thank you for being a part of my life and the community of Intentionalism. You make this book and journey possible.

Made in the USA
Columbia, SC
31 May 2023

fd565b4a-e497-4434-958c-5b389a322b0fR01